Intermediate
VOCABULARY
Games

Jill Hadfield

Longman

photocopiable material

Pearson Education Limited
Edinburgh Gate
Harlow
Essex CM20 2JE
England
and Associated Companies throughout the World.
longman.com

First published 1999
Second impression 2001
ISBN: 0582 339308

Printed in Spain by Mateu Cromo

Produced for the Publishers by Geneviève Talon
Designer: Trevor Sylvester, TSGD
Copy editor: Liz Hornby
Illustrated by: Gabrielle Morton (units 1, 5, 13, 17, 18, 20, 21, 22);
Nick Abadzis (units 2, 7, 9, 11, 26, 30); John Plumb (units 3, 6, 12,
15, 19, 25, 27); Andy Warrington (units 4, 8, 10, 16, 23, 24, 29)

I am very grateful to colleagues and students
from the EFL section of South Devon
College for their inspiration and help, and to
Liz Hornby and Geneviève Talon for their
patient and skilful editing.

Jill Hadfield

Contents

Introduction 4

Teacher's notes

1	Transport	7
2	Entertainment	8
3	Restaurants	9
4	Illness	10
5	Cookery	11
6	Animals	12
7	School and university subjects	14
8	Sports	14
9	Tools and DIY	15
10	Office objects	16
11	Computers	17
12	Actions (1)	18
13	Actions (2)	19
14	Approval and disapproval	19
15	People	20
16	Colours and shapes	21
17	Scenery	23
18	Sounds	24
19	Sensations	25
20	Emotions	26
21	Personality	27
22	Travel	28
23	Television	29
24	Holidays	30
25	Work	31
26	Crime	32
27	The law	34
28	Education	35
29	Relationships	36
30	Space	37

Games material 39

Rules sheets 142

Introduction

1 About games

A game is an activity with rules, a goal and an element of fun. There are two kinds of games: *competitive games*, in which players or teams race to be the first to reach the goal, and *cooperative games*, in which players or teams work together towards a common goal.

The activities in this book fall into two further categories: *linguistic games* and *communicative games*. In linguistic games, the goal of the game is linguistic accuracy: in the case of these vocabulary games, remembering the correct word. Communicative games have a goal or aim that is not linguistic: successful completion of the game involves carrying out a task such as exchanging information, filling in a picture or chart, or finding two matching cards, rather than the correct production of language. However, in order to carry out this task it will be necessary to use language and, by careful construction of the task, it is possible to specify in advance what language will be required.

These games can be used at all stages of the progression from controlled to free practice, serving at one end of the range as a memory aid and repetition drill, and at the other as a chance to use language freely and as a means to an end rather than an end in itself. They can also serve as a diagnostic tool for the teacher, who can note areas of difficulty and take appropriate remedial action.

2 About vocabulary

I started writing vocabulary games books because I was interested in the process of acquiring vocabulary, i.e. the processes that go on *after* the introduction and explanation of new vocabulary. How do we remember new words? How do we expect our students to remember them? How can a new word or a set of new words become integrated into our existing word store? How can we become so familiar with it that we can locate it and pull it out again when we need to use it?

Remembering new words is hard. Words are slippery things: before you know it, they've wriggled away and are gone. It takes a lot of effort to keep them where you want them. It seems to me that in order to retain a word, students have to go through three distinct processes. They have to fix the meaning of the word in their minds; they have somehow to make the word their own – to personalise it so that it takes on a colour and a character for them and becomes part of their individual word store – and they have to use the word creatively in context for themselves.

The question for me, in writing these books, was firstly: How could I devise activities that would help the learner through these three processes?
(1) Fix the meaning of the word in your mind.
(2) Make the word your own.
(3) Use the word to communicate with others.
And secondly: How could I make it fun?

3 About this book

This is the second in a series of resource books of practice activities for vocabulary: the games have been designed to **practise**, not to introduce, new vocabulary. The book assumes that introduction and explanation of the vocabulary has been done in the textbook or other course material that the teacher and class is following.

This book differs slightly from *Elementary Vocabulary Games*, in that it is aimed at addressing the particular needs of intermediate learners. The lexical areas covered begin to depart from the elementary field of concrete nouns and everyday vocabulary to include more abstractions and vocabulary centred around more complex topics. Intermediate learners need more abstract or descriptive vocabulary to talk about such things as feelings and sensations or to describe objects or scenery. They also begin to want to use their language to discuss issues of interest. About one third of the units cover concrete, everyday, or situational vocabulary (e.g. Transport, Illness) and are of a level similar to the units towards the end of the elementary book, one third cover more abstract and descriptive vocabulary (e.g. Sensations, Emotions), and one third cover issues and complex topics (e.g. Crime, Education).

The materials are graded within the book, those towards the end using more complex language and containing game and role cards with short reading texts to reflect the intermediate student's need for more reading material.

The vocabulary items have been arranged in lexical sets following topics used in most textbooks and courses at this level. The topic area, vocabulary focus, structures and any extra vocabulary (not the main focus) that the students will need are all listed at the start of the teacher's notes. Structures are those that a student at this stage could reasonably be expected to know.

As in *Elementary Vocabulary Games*, each unit has three games, taking the student through the three processes described above: (1) **memorising**, (2) **personalising** and (3) **communicating**. The three stages are self-contained, so that the teacher is free to select or discard any game, according to what she feels her students need; they are all different in nature and make use of different game techniques.

Games 1, 2 and 3

Game 1 in each unit is a **memorising** game, designed to fix the meaning of the word in the student's mind. These games are linguistic games as distinct from the other two games in the unit which focus on communication; their focus is on accuracy rather than fluency and often they only require the student to produce single words or phrases rather than sentences. The games used in this stage are very simple versions of matching (including lotto games), labelling, sorting, ordering, guessing (including mime games), arranging and collecting. In each case, the aim of the game is to get the students to remember and produce the right word (matching words to pictures for example, or guessing which word is being mimed, or sorting words into two lexical sets).

Game 2, **personalising** – these are not really games, but activities designed to get the students to relate the new words to their personal experience. They comprise two phases: a reflective phase, where students are asked to visualise something or associate the words with their personal life and preferences (sometimes filling in a questionnaire), and a communicative phase where they are asked to discuss what they have thought or written with others. The language in this stage is also fairly controlled (sentence patterns and frames are often given), though the students will now need to produce whole utterances, not single words.

In Game 3, **communicating**, the focus is on successful completion of a goal such as finding a person, solving a puzzle or completing a drawing, rather than on correct production of lexis and structures. In this stage, language is less controlled and more flexibility and creativity are required of the students. The whole range of communicative games is included: matching, searching, information gap, role-play, arranging and ordering, and exchanging and collecting games.

Types of game
The games make use of a variety of techniques, variety being important in language teaching. The simplest games are *sorting*, *ordering*, or *arranging* games. These are usually played in pairs, where students sort cards into different groups of vocabulary, e.g. public transport and private transport.

In *information gap* games, Player 1 has access to some information not held by Player 2. Player 2 must acquire this information to complete a task successfully. This type of game may be *one-sided* or *reciprocal*, where both players have information which they must pool to solve a common problem. The games may be played in pairs or small groups, where all members of the group have some information.

Guessing games are a familiar variant on this principle. The player with the information deliberately withholds it, while others guess what it might be.

Search games are another variant, involving the whole class. In these games everyone in the class has one piece of information. Players must obtain all or a large amount of the information available to fill in a chart or picture or to solve a problem. Each student is thus simultaneously a giver and a collector of information.

Matching games are based on a different principle, but also involve a transfer of information. These involve matching corresponding pairs of cards or pictures, and may be played as a whole class activity, where everyone must circulate until they find a partner with a corresponding card or picture, or a pairwork or small group activity, played as a card game on either the 'snap' or the 'pelmanism' principle.

Labelling games involve matching labels to items in a picture.

Exchanging games are based on the 'barter' principle. Players have certain articles, cards or ideas which they wish to exchange for others. The aim of the game is to make an exchange which is satisfactory to both sides.

Exchanging and collecting games are an extension of this. Players have certain articles or cards which they are willing to exchange for others in order to complete a set. This may be played as a whole class activity, where players circulate freely, exchanging articles or cards at random; or as a card game on the 'rummy' principle.

Board games and *card games* are familiar game types, where the aim is to be the first round a board, or to collect the most cards, or to get rid of the cards first, or to build up a story. The cards and squares on the board are used as stimuli to provoke a communication exchange.

All the above activities may include elements of role-play or of simulation.

In *role-play* games, players are given the name and some characteristics of a fictional character. These are not role-plays in the true sense, as the role-play element is always subordinate to the use of language. The outcome of a game is 'closed'; once cards are distributed it develops in a certain predetermined way, while role-play proper is open-ended and may develop in any number of ways.

4 Practical considerations
Classroom management
There are three main types of activities in this book: *pairwork*, involving two partners, *small group work*, involving groups of three or four, and *whole class activities*, where everyone moves freely around the room. All these activities require some flexibility in the constitution of groups and organisation of the classroom. It is best to have the desks or tables in a U-shape if possible. Students can then work with the person sitting next to them for pairwork, and groups of threes and fours can easily be constituted by alternate pairs moving their chairs to the inner side of the U, opposite another pair. Whole class activities, which involve all the students circulating freely, can take place in the empty area in the centre of the U-shape. If it is not possible to arrange desks in this way, this need not deter you: the traditional arrangement of front-facing desks can be easily adapted to pairwork, with people at adjoining desks working together, while small groups can be formed by two people turning their chairs round to face the people behind them. Whole class activities present a little more of a problem, but often there is a space big enough for the students to move around in at the front of the class, or desks can be pushed back to clear a space in the centre.

Sometimes an alternative small group version of the whole class games in this book has been provided, so that teachers who experience a great deal of difficulty with the kind of games that require students to move around can play these games in a more static format.

Games are best set up by demonstration rather than by lengthy explanation. The teacher should explain briefly what the game involves, hand out the photocopied cards, make sure students have pen and paper if needed, give them a little time to study the cards, and then demonstrate the game with one of the students in front of the class.

It will be found that the idea of the game is probably easier for students to grasp from seeing the cards than from a verbal explanation, and that as they become more familiar with the idea of the games and the techniques used, any initial problems caused by unfamiliarity will quickly disappear. Where more complicated card games are played in small groups, a Rules sheet is provided and it is suggested that teachers hand out a photocopy of this to each group of students together with the cards. These games are indicated in the Teacher's notes with the symbol RULES SHEET .

Role-play games involve two distinct phases: preparation and production. In the preparation phase students should be given sufficient time to digest the information on the role card and to ask the teacher for help with anything they do not understand. When the students are sufficiently prepared, and all the problems of comprehension are ironed out, the role-play can begin. Encourage the students not to rely too heavily on looking at their role cards, but to remember the information. With the shorter role cards it is a good idea to collect them in before the role-play begins.

The teacher's role in all these activities is that of monitor and resource centre, moving from group to group, listening, supplying any necessary language, noting errors, but not interrupting or correcting as this impedes fluency and spoils the atmosphere. It is a good idea to carry paper and pen and to note any persistent errors or areas of difficulty. These can then be dealt with in a feedback session after the game. In many cases the game could then be played again with different partners or with different role cards.

The average length of time for the games in the book is about 15 to 20 minutes. All three games in each unit could therefore be played in an average lesson. In some units, Game 3 may take a little longer (30 minutes or so) and this has been indicated in the Teacher's notes with the symbol Long game .

Answers to games are provided in three ways: some are printed in the Teacher's notes; some are shown when cards are copied back-to-back (see opposite); and some (*not* the pages for back-to-back copying) can be seen by looking at two pages side by side, where matching cards will appear in the same position on each page.

Amending the games: If you don't feel your students need to practise all the words listed for any unit, simply select the cards you feel most appropriate for their level or culture. But if you use fewer cards, make sure the number and type of cards you choose will be enough to play the game properly (for example, ensure that you discard picture and word cards that correspond, or all the cards in any one category).

Resource management

The resources required for each game fall into two categories: reusable and disposable. Where a very small number of photocopies are needed for a whole class game or where students may write on their cards, it is best to treat these photocopies as disposable, and there is no point in collecting up the photocopies in order to use them with another class when the game is finished.

In contrast, most of the games require a larger number of copies and an investment of the teacher's time in accurate copying, cutting up and sorting, so it is worthwhile thinking of these materials as reusable resources. For example, Game 1 in most units requires a set of cards for each pair of students in the class. The students will not need to write anything on the cards, and as these are mostly quiet games with only two people involved, the cards should reach the end of the game in much the same state as they began. So it is worth investing some time in making the photocopies into a permanent class set of materials. If you have the time and resources, obviously printing or pasting the materials onto card or laminating them would help preserve their shelf-life. However, this isn't absolutely necessary – I have sets of games materials printed only onto paper that have done their duty in workshops all over the world and aren't much the worse for wear after several years. What is more important is providing a system to prevent the materials getting lost and disorganised. If you have a class set of ten packs of cards, for example, it is worth putting each pack into an envelope clearly labelled with the name of the game and the number of cards. It is then the students' responsibility to collect up all the cards at the end of the game, check that they are all there, put them back into the envelope and hand them back to you. If two packs of cards are required for a game, keep them in two smaller envelopes inside the big one, and get the students to sort them back into their respective envelopes at the end of the game.

Some pages of cards, marked with the symbol ⟷ at the top, are intended for **back-to-back photocopying**, where for example cards will have a picture on one side and the corresponding word on the other. If your copier will do back-to-back, this should present no problem, although you will have to be fairly careful about aligning the sheets. If you cannot print back-to-back, there are two solutions: (1) make two sets of cards, one with pictures and one with words. This means that you will have to adapt the games with the picture/word cards into simpler matching games as in Game 1 in unit 9, *Tools and DIY*. This solution obviously restricts the range of games available to you, so it is better in the long run to adopt solution (2): write the words on the backs yourself, or, better still, get the students to do it – this could form part of a vocabulary practice exercise, although you will have to check they've done it correctly: when back-to-back photocopying is indicated, matching cards will appear in the sequence A B C D across each row of one page and in the sequence D C B A across each row of the other page.

Finally, if you have no access to copying facilities at all, it is possible, though time-consuming, to make home-made versions of the materials by getting the students to work with you to draw and write the cards.

Teacher's notes

1 Transport

Topic area
forms of transport

Vocabulary focus
public transport: *ferry, coach, bus, taxi, tram, plane, train, tube/underground*

personal transport: *car, bike, motorbike, caravan*

goods vehicles: *lorry, van*

emergency vehicles: *ambulance, fire engine*

places: *railway station, airport, bus stop, coach station, ferry terminal, taxi rank, tram stop, tube/underground station, lorry/van depot, fire station, hospital, garage, bike stand, motorcycle bay, caravan park*

Structures
present continuous (*I'm looking for …*), *can you tell me where the … is?, I've (never) been …*

Materials and preparation
GAME 1 Copy and cut up one set of VEHICLES cards and one set of PLACES cards per pair of students. Don't forget the words on the back of the VEHICLES cards.

GAME 2 None.

GAME 3 Copy and cut up one set of VEHICLES picture cards (public transport only, above the solid rule) and one set of PLACES cards (public transport only) per two students. They can play with or without the words on the back of the VEHICLES cards. Divide the public transport cards into two groups of four cards, and keep them separate.

How to use the games
GAME 1 Memorising
1 pairwork sorting game
- Divide students into pairs and give each pair a set of VEHICLES cards.

- Get them to spread these out word-side up.

- **The object of the game is to sort them into four piles: *public transport*, *personal transport*, *goods vehicles* and *emergency vehicles*.**

- The students should see how quickly they can do this.

- They can check, when they have finished, by looking at the pictures.

2 small group matching game
- Then put each pair of students together with another pair to make a group of four.

- Give each group a set of PLACES cards.

- They should shuffle together and deal out their two sets of vehicles cards and put the place cards face down in a pile in the middle of the table.

- **The object of the game is to match place and vehicle.**

- They take it in turns to turn up a card from the pile of place cards. The player who turns up the place card should not show it to the others but ask a question, e.g. *'What would you see in a railway station?'*

- The player who gives the right answer, producing the correct vehicle card from her hand first (*'A train!'*) can lay down the card.

- At the end the player with fewest cards in her hand is the winner.

GAME 2 Personalising
pairwork discussion
- Ask students to write a list of the forms of transport they have used.

- Then put them in pairs to compare lists: *'I've been on/in a …' 'I've never been on/in a …'*.

GAME 3 Communicating
whole class exchanging and collecting game
Getting there
- Give each student four of the eight *public transport* VEHICLES cards.

- Tell them they have to make a very long and complicated journey involving these forms of transport. They should number their cards in the order they plan to make their journey.

- Give each student four of the eight *public transport* PLACES cards. (These should *not* correspond to their transport cards.)

- **The object of the game is for every player to find place cards for his vehicles cards.**

- Tell them they must find out where their transport leaves from.

- For example, if the picture they have labelled 1 is a picture of a train, they must find the railway station by asking other students, *'Excuse me. I'm looking for the railway station. Do you know where it is?'*

7

- If the student they ask has a railway station card he should give it to them, saying, *'Right here!'* or *'Right in front of you!'* If not, they have to go on asking. They must find the places in the order they have decided to plan their journey.

- When they have obtained the place cards they want and given away those they don't want, they can sit down.

- Or: the student who completes his journey first is the winner.

2 Entertainment

Topic area
entertainment and social life

Vocabulary focus
places: *theatre, cinema, concert hall, opera house, dance hall/ballroom, disco, pub, restaurant*

events: *play, film, meal, drink, ballet, concert (classical/ rock/pop/folk), disco, dance, opera*

people: *barman, waiters, actors, film stars, dancers, musicians, disc jockey, band, singers*

Structures
simple present, *like/hate + -ing, would like, going to, I think/imagine (that)*

Materials and preparation

GAME 1 Copy and cut up one complete set of PLACES, PEOPLE and EVENTS cards per pair of students. Don't forget the words on the back. You could also provide one paper bag per pair of students.

GAME 2 None.

GAME 3 Copy the TICKETS AND VOUCHERS twice for one third of the number of students (e.g. 20 sheets for 30 students). Cut them up and give students two tickets/vouchers each for three events (e.g. two tickets for the play, the opera and the film).

NOTE: If you don't feel your students need to practise all the words, simply select the cards you feel most appropriate for their level/culture. In Game 1, you can limit the vocabulary either by using only two sets of cards instead of three (PLACES and EVENTS, for example, leaving out PEOPLE) or by using fewer cards in each set. If you use fewer cards in each set, make sure the cards you choose match up. (If you choose to teach 'theatre', for example, you will have to include the cards for 'play' and 'actors' as well.) In Game 3, simply choose the tickets/vouchers you feel are most suitable.

How to use the games
GAME 1 Memorising
pairwork sorting game
- Divide students into pairs.

- Give each pair a set of PLACES, PEOPLE and EVENTS cards.

- **The object of the game is to match up places with people and events.**

- The students should put the place cards word-side up in a pile in the middle of the table and spread out the events and people cards word-side up. (They may like to cover the pile with a piece of paper, so they cannot see which word is coming up next. Alternatively, they could put the place cards in a paper bag and use it as a 'lucky dip'.)

- They should take it in turns to take a card from the place pile (sliding it out from under the paper) or dip into the bag and take a card.

- The first to identify the event and people connected with each place (e.g. theatre – play – actors) can keep the cards. (If two students pick up cards simultaneously they can keep one card each.)

- The player with most cards at the end is the winner.

- They can check their answers by turning over the cards to see the pictures.

- Then they can replay the game in the same way, but this time with all the cards picture-side up, so that they have to remember the words. This time the rule is that they must say all three words (e.g. cinema – film – film stars) before they are allowed to pick up the cards.

GAME 2 Personalising
pairwork discussion
- Put up the following headings on the board:

  I LIKE GOING TO
  I QUITE LIKE GOING TO
  I DON'T LIKE GOING TO

- Ask students to start by working on their own, copying these column headings on to a piece of paper.

- Then write the following phrases in random order on the board (or if students still have the PLACES and EVENTS cards from Game 1 they could spread these out picture-side up on the table):

  the theatre, the ballet, the opera, the cinema, discos, classical music concerts, rock concerts, folk concerts, pop concerts, dances, pubs, restaurants.

- Students should complete their columns with phrases chosen from the selection.

- Then put them in pairs and ask them to guess each other's choices:

  A: *'You like going to pubs, don't you?'*

  B: *'How did you guess?'*

GAME 3 Communicating
whole class exchanging game
Ticketswap

- Give students two TICKETS/VOUCHERS each for three different events (six tickets or vouchers in total).

- Tell them they have been given these tickets/vouchers for events next week. Ask them to put dates on the tickets in the blank space after the specified day.

- The vouchers for the disco and restaurant can be used on any day and can be used on the same day as any other event: students can go on to the disco after the film, for example, or out to a meal after the folk concert.

- **The object of the game is for students to find someone to go with them to each of the three events.**

- To do this, they will have to get up and move around the class, asking people if they would like to come with them, e.g.

  A: *'I've got two tickets for the theatre on Monday night. Would you like to come with me?'*

  B: *'Sorry! I'm going out myself that night. But I've got an extra ticket for a folk concert on Friday. Do you fancy coming? It's Devonair.'*

- Students can accept or refuse on the basis of their own preferences and whether they are already going out that night. (The game will get more frantic as it goes on!)

- They should try to get rid of their three spare tickets/vouchers and get three new ones (i.e. they should end up with six different tickets/vouchers). You can set a time limit for this if you like.

NOTES: 1. If you want to make the game less competitive or less frantic, you can specify that the events are all this month, instead of next week. (It might lose a bit of its zest, though.)

2. If you want a more static version of the game, with students sitting in groups instead of moving around, put students in groups of 3–4 and give each member of the group two different pairs of tickets (for groups of four) or three different pairs of tickets (for groups of three.) The object of the game then is for the group to arrange things so that all the tickets are used and everyone is doing something on every night of the week. (It may help to ask them to draw up a diary page for next week, showing who is going where and with whom.)

GRAMMAR NOTE: The correct use of articles is often a source of confusion for students, and when talking about leisure activities and entertainment there are some specific points to note.

A general rule to follow is that when we are talking about a specific production (an '**event**'), we use phrases with 'a' (e.g. *a play, a ballet, an opera*):
I'm going to a play tonight.
I went to a ballet last week which was wonderful.
Susan is taking me to see an opera tomorrow.

When we talk about a type of entertainment (or a '**place**'), we use phrases with 'the' (e.g. *the theatre, the cinema*):
We want to go to the cinema, but we haven't decided what film to see.
We're going to the theatre tonight, but I don't know what play is on.

But note that some 'places' cannot represent a type of entertainment in this way. For example, we don't say: 'We're going to the concert hall/opera house/the dance hall/the ballroom', but instead:
We're going to a concert.
We're going to the opera.
We're going to the ballet.
We're going dancing.

Note too that we use 'a' with *meal* and *drink*:
We're going for a meal in town and then meeting John for a drink.

3 Restaurants

Topic area
meals and drinks

Vocabulary focus
general: *starter, main course, dessert, menu*

cooking methods: *grilled, roast, stir-fried, boiled, mashed, jacket, curry, stew*

starters: *avocado, melon, prawn cocktail, soup*

main courses: (meat and fish:) *beef, lamb, pork, ham, chicken, chops, steak, fish, cod, plaice*; (starch:) *pasta, rice, chips*; (vegetables:) *potatoes, peas, carrots, cauliflower, courgettes, green beans, salad*

desserts: *ice cream, chocolate mousse, cheesecake, apple pie, strawberry tart, yoghurt, fruit, cheese*

drinks: *beer, (house) wine, gin and tonic, sherry, cider, whisky, brandy, lemonade, orange juice, mineral water*

Extra vocabulary
medium, well done, rare

Structures
be, simple present, *would like, let's … /shall we … / how about … , could I have… please*

Materials and preparation

GAME 1 Copy and cut up one complete set (1 and 2) of FOOD AND DRINK cards per pair of students. (42 cards: pictures with words on the back.) You could also provide one paper bag for every four students.

GAME 2 Same cards as Game 1.

GAME 3 Two complete sets of FOOD AND DRINK cards (84 cards) and one MENU per pair.

NOTE: If you don't feel your students need to learn all the words, simply select the cards you feel most appropriate for their level/culture. Beef, ham, pork and alcohol are sensitive items in some cultures (although students whose religion forbids these may still need to know the vocabulary if they are travelling to an English-speaking country – in order to refuse them). The cards in Game 1 and the menu in Game 3 are based on standard British/European food, but it is perfectly possible to make your own menu and additional cards for these games to reflect your students' culture and cuisine.

How to use the games
GAME 1 Memorising
1 pairwork sorting game
- Divide students into pairs.

- Give each pair a set of the 42 FOOD AND DRINK cards.

- Ask them to shuffle them and then spread them out on the table word-side up.

- **The object of the game is to sort them into two groups:** *food* **and** *drink*.

- When they have done this they can sort the food items out into *starter, main course* and *dessert*.

- They can check if they are right by turning over the cards to see the pictures.

- When all the cards are picture-side up, they can see if they can remember all the names.

Make this into a competition if you like:

2 small group matching game
- Join up the pairs with another pair.

- Get them to collect one set of cards into a pile and place them picture-side up, and to spread the other set out word-side up.

- Conceal the picture pile in some way so that the players cannot see the top card, either by placing a sheet of paper over the top or putting the set of cards in a paper bag.

- The players take it in turns to take a card from the pile (or out of the bag) and hold it up.

- **The object of the game is to match words and pictures.**

- The first player to find and say the matching word can keep both cards.

- The player with most cards at the end is the winner.

GAME 2 Personalising
pairwork discussion
- Put students in pairs and give them a set of the 42 FOOD AND DRINK cards.

- Ask them to spread these out word-side up so that they can both read them.

- Ask them to choose a meal that they would like from the items on the cards and write it down.

- Then ask them to choose a meal that they think their partner would like and write it down.

- Then get them to compare their lists – did they choose well?

GAME 3 Communicating   `Long game`
whole class race
Fast food
- Divide the class into roughly two thirds and one third. Make sure the two-thirds group is an even number.

- Ask two thirds of the students to sit in pairs at tables. They are the customers. Give each pair a MENU.

- Further divide the smaller group into waiters and kitchen staff.

- The waiters should have pen and paper. Assign each waiter an equal number of customers each.

- Put the kitchen staff in front of a table and give them two sets of FOOD AND DRINK pictures. Ask them to spread the 84 pictures out on the table behind them.

- (E.g. for a group of 17 you might have 12 customers sitting in pairs at 6 tables, 3 waiters in charge of 2 tables each and 2 kitchen staff in front of a table.)

- **The object of the game is for the waiters to take the customers' orders and obtain the items from the kitchen staff.**

- The waiter and customers who finish first are the winners.

RULES
1. The waiters can only take orders from one person at a time.

2. If the kitchen staff run out of an item the waiter must go back and get an alternative order from the customer.

3. The waiters may not see the items available in the kitchen.

4 Illness

Topic area
health

Vocabulary focus
ailments: *cold, cough, sore throat, headache, earache, toothache, stomach ache, rash, backache, flu, temperature, swollen, pain, black eye, burn/burnt, lost my voice, broken, cut, sprain/sprained, feel sick, hurts, bruise*

people: *doctor, dentist, nurse, patient*

remedies: *antibiotics, aspirin, antiseptic cream/ointment, throat sweets, cough medicine, plaster, bandage, injection, hospital, X-ray, go home, lie down, ice pack, stitches*

general: *accident-prone, injury, healthy*

Extra vocabulary

terrible, serious, awful; parts of the body

Structures

have got, simple present (*I feel ... , my ... hurts*),
need a ... , need to, should/ought to, present perfect
(*I've lost my voice*)

Materials and preparation

GAME 1 Copy and cut up one set of AILMENTS WORDS.

GAME 2 Make one copy of the HEALTH QUESTIONNAIRE
for each student in the class.

GAME 3 Copy and cut up one set of AILMENTS PICTURES
and one set of REMEDIES cards for each group of 3–4
students.

How to use the games

GAME 1 Memorising
whole class guessing game

- Divide students into two teams.

- Give each team a set of AILMENTS WORDS.

- These two piles should be placed face down on a
  table at the front.

- Tell the teams you are a patient and they are (1)
  doctors and (2) nurses. Can they see what is wrong
  with you? Mime *'I've lost my voice'*.

- When they have guessed, e.g. *'Have you got a sore
  throat?'* *'Have you lost your voice?'*, get one student
  from each team to come to the front.

- Tell the teams this is a new patient who has also lost
  his voice. What else is wrong with him?

- The new patient should take the next card from his
  team's pile and mime the ailment.

- **The object of the game is for each team to guess
  from the 'patient's' mime what is wrong.**

- When someone guesses correctly they should come
  and get the next card.

- The team which finishes first is the winner.

GAME 2 Personalising
pairwork discussion

- Give a copy of the HEALTH QUESTIONNAIRE to
  each student.

- Get them to fill it in individually.

- Then put them in pairs to compare their answers.

GAME 3 Communicating
small group matching game
The NHS

RULES SHEET

- Divide students into groups of 3–4.

- Give each group a set of AILMENTS PICTURES and a set
  of REMEDIES cards.

- They should put the ailments cards face down in a
  pile in the middle of the table and deal out the
  remedies cards.

- Each player can look at his remedies cards, but should
  not show them to the others.

- The first player begins by picking up an ailments card
  and describing what's wrong, as if he were a patient.
  (E.g. *'I've got a terrible headache'*, *'I think my arm is
  broken'*, etc.)

- The others should compete to offer solutions,
  according to the remedies they hold in their hands:
  'You should take an aspirin', *'You need to go home and
  lie down'*, *'You need an X-ray'*, etc.

- The 'patient' can select the most suitable remedy.
  If nothing acceptable is offered, he can replace the
  card at the bottom of the pile. (Patients cannot treat
  themselves!)

- **The object of the game is for the 'doctors' to
  get rid of all their remedies.**

- The doctor who gets rid of his remedies first is
  the winner.

5 Cookery

Topic area
cooking

Vocabulary focus

cooking methods: *heat, prepare, fry, roast, boil, bake,
grill, simmer, mix, add, stir, beat, grate, chop, mash,
blend, weigh, sieve, peel, season, dice, whisk*

equipment and utensils: *oven, frying pan, cake tin,
roasting tin, saucepan, grill pan, (wooden) spoon, fork,
grater, whisk, knife, masher, blender, mixer, scales, sieve,
peeler, saltcellar, pepper mill*

Extra vocabulary

common food items (e.g. *flour, sugar, onion*); *ounce (oz),
pound (lb), pint; remove, turn, turn out, pour, reheat,
sprinkle, slide, place; bowl, ingredients, degrees, bone;
dried, greased, smooth, liquid, solid, melted, hot, cool*

Structures

imperatives, *have got, need*

Materials and preparation

GAME 1 Copy one set of COOKING cards (with words on the back) and one set of UTENSILS cards for each pair of students in your class.

GAME 2 None.

GAME 3 Copy and cut up one RECIPES sheet and one UTENSILS sheet for every four students. Keep each recipe separate from its corresponding utensils: the first four rows of utensils each correspond to the same-numbered recipe.

How to use the games

GAME 1 Memorising

1 pairwork sorting game

• Divide your class into pairs.

• Give each pair a set of COOKING cards.

• Get them to lay them out word-side up and sort them into two groups: *preparing food* and *heating food*.

• They can check by looking at the pictures.

• When the cards are all picture-side up, they can test themselves to see if they can remember the words.

2 pairwork matching game

• Then give each pair a complete set of 20 UTENSILS cards.

• Get them to put these in a pile, face down.

• They should spread the COOKING cards out word-side up.

• The players should take it in turns to turn up a card from the pile.

• **The object of the game is to match the actions on the cooking cards with the utensils needed.**

• The player who can do this first (e.g. *'You need scales to weigh food'*, *'You need a knife to dice food'*) can keep the cards.

• The player with most cards at the end is the winner.

NOTE: The UTENSILS cards have both word and picture. You can make the game harder by giving students words only (cut the pictures off).

GAME 2 Personalising

pairwork guessing game

• Ask students to think of their favourite dish and to write down how it is made (or how they think it's made if they're not cookery experts!).

• Get them to read their recipes to a partner without saying the name of the dish.

• If you have a monolingual class, the partner should try to guess the name of the dish. If they are a multicultural class, they can simply share recipes.

GAME 3 Communicating

whole class exchanging and collecting game
Ready Steady Cook

• Give each student a RECIPE card.

• Mix up the UTENSILS cards you have copied and give them out so that each student gets different utensils from the ones required in their recipe.

• **The object of the game is to collect the four utensils cards needed for the recipe.**

• To do this they will have to read their recipe, work out what four utensils they need, and go round the class asking other students if they can give them what they need, e.g. *'I need a grater. Have you got one?'*

NOTES: 1. If you want to make this game harder, cut the words off the bottom of the UTENSILS cards and give them pictures only.

2. If you want to reinforce the cooking verbs but not practise utensil vocabulary, get them to ask for the utensil they need by saying, *'I need something for ...ing'* or *'I need something to ... with'*.

6 Animals

Topic area
animal names

Vocabulary focus
pets: *cat, dog, rabbit, hamster, parrot, canary, guinea pig, mouse, goldfish*

wild animals: *lion, tiger, elephant, hippo, rhino, crocodile, snake, zebra, camel, bear, frog, seal, kangaroo, tortoise*

farm animals: *chicken, sheep, cow, horse, pig, duck, goat, goose*

Extra vocabulary
adjectives for describing character (e.g. *happy, friendly, talkative*); words for classifying animals (e.g. *farm animals, reptiles, pets, wild animals, birds, eat grass, eat meat, stripes, fur*)

Structures
have got, simple present (*I think ...*), *because ...*

Materials and preparation

GAME 1 Copy and cut up one set of ANIMALS WORDS and two sets of ANIMALS PICTURES per group of 3–4 students. Cut one of the sheets of ANIMALS PICTURES into individual pictures and the other into four LOTTO BOARDS, each containing six pictures. (Discard the seven pictures at the bottom.) You will also need one paper bag per group.

GAME 2 None.

GAME 3 Copy and cut up one set of ANIMALS PICTURES per group of 3–4 students.

___

How to use the games

GAME 1 Memorising

1 small group guessing game

• Divide students into groups of 3–4 and give each group a set of ANIMALS WORDS.

• Ask them to place them in a pile, face down.

• They should take it in turns to take a card from the pile, without showing it to the others.

• The student who is taking the card from the pile must either mime or draw that animal.

• **The object of the game is for the rest of the group to guess the animal from the mime/drawing.**

• The group that gets through the pile fastest is the winner.

2 small group lotto game

• Give each group three or four LOTTO BOARDS, one for each member of the group, and a set of ANIMALS PICTURES in a paper bag.

• One student should take a card from the bag. Carefully keeping it hidden from the others, she should look at the picture and say the name of the animal.

• The student who has that picture on the board should ask for the picture and put it on the board.

• **The object of the game is to fill your board first.**

NOTE: Some of the ANIMALS PICTURES don't appear on the boards: *hamster, canary, guinea pig, seal, goat, goose, kangaroo.* You can either remove these before the game starts, or tell the students that some animals do not appear on the boards.

GAME 2 Personalising

pairwork discussion

• Elicit from the students some adjectives they associate with animals, e.g. dog – *happy, friendly*; cat – *independent*; mouse – *quiet, timid*; parrot – *noisy, talkative*; lion – *brave*; tortoise – *slow, lazy*.

• Provide some of your own and put these up on the board.

• Tell the students about your 'animal family', e.g. *'My father is a bit like a dog – he's always happy and friendly. My brother is like a tortoise in the morning – he moves very slowly and won't get out of bed! I think my older sister is really a parrot – always talking!'*

• Ask students to close their eyes and think about all the people in their (extended) families and to decide what kind of animals they would be. Give them some time to visualise and then write down their ideas.

• When they have finished they can discuss their ideas with their partner; or you can ask for contributions from the whole class.

GAME 3 Communicating

small group collecting game

RULES SHEET

Animal families

• Divide students into groups of 3–4 and give each a set of ANIMALS PICTURES.

• Ask them to spread these out on the table.

• Write up on the board:

PETS   WILD ANIMALS   FARM ANIMALS

• Ask groups to sort the cards as quickly as possible into these three groups.

• Then write the following categories on the board too. As you write, ask the students to give you an example for each category:

ANIMALS THAT EAT MEAT
ANIMALS THAT EAT GRASS
ANIMALS   BIRDS   REPTILES
ANIMALS THAT LIVE IN THE AIR / IN THE WATER / ON THE LAND
CATS
ANIMALS WITH STRIPES
ANIMALS WITH FUR

• Leave the headings on the board for reference.

• Then ask one person in each group to shuffle and deal out five cards to each player and put the rest face down in the middle of the table.

• They should not show their cards to the other players.

• **The object of the game is to collect sets of three animals.** These 'sets' can be grouped on any basis, e.g. lion, tiger, cat are all *cats*; hamster, cat, dog are all *pets*; canary, parrot, duck are all *birds*; lion, tiger, dog all *eat meat*; tiger, zebra, snake all have *stripes*, etc.

• The players should look at their cards and group together any sets of three that they have already. When it comes to their turn (but not before) they can lay these down on the table, justifying their grouping, e.g. *'I have a seal, a goldfish and a frog. They all live in water.'*

• Player 1 begins by laying down any sets she has in her hand and justifying them. Then she can try to complete her other sets by choosing one other player and asking for a card to complete her set, e.g. *'Anna, have you got any animals that eat grass?'* If the answer is yes, she can collect the card from Anna and lay down the set if it is complete, justifying it as above. If the answer is no, or if she has no cards left in her hand after laying down the set, she can pick up a card from the pile. Then the turn passes to the next player.

• The winner is the person with most sets at the end.

7 School and university subjects

Topic area
school and university subjects

Vocabulary focus
literature, drama, history, geography, music, physics, chemistry, philosophy, religious education/theology, biology, mathematics/maths, politics, psychology, art, P.E.

Structures
I like(d), I don't/didn't like ... , my favourite/least favourite subject is/was ... , What's your name?, What subject are you studying?

Materials and preparation

GAME 1 Copy and cut up one set of BOOKS cards, and copy one LIBRARY PLAN, for each pair of students. Don't forget to copy the SUBJECTS on the back of the BOOKS cards.

GAME 2 Make one copy of the TIMETABLE for each pair, or a large copy on OHP or blackboard that everyone can see.

GAME 3

- *If you have fewer than 15 students:* Make one copy of the HALL OF RESIDENCE PLAN, and one sheet of REGISTRATION FORMS. Work out which REGISTRATION FORMS you are going to use for your students. Write in the names from the others that you are not going to use on the appropriate doors on the copy of the PLAN. Then use this as your copy master. Make one copy of your adapted HALL OF RESIDENCE PLAN for each student. Cut up one REGISTRATION FORM for each student.

- *If you have 15 students:* Make one copy of the HALL OF RESIDENCE PLAN for each student in the class. Copy one sheet of REGISTRATION FORMS and cut up one FORM for each student.

- *If you have more than 15 students:* Some people will have to share rooms! Copy one HALL OF RESIDENCE PLAN for each student and make enough copies of the sheet of REGISTRATION FORMS to give one FORM to each student. Keep the first 15 forms exactly as they are, but put new names on the rest.

How to use the games
GAME 1 Memorising
pairwork arranging game
- Divide the students into pairs.

- Give each pair a set of BOOKS cards.

- Get them to spread these out picture-side up on the desk.

- Ask them to imagine they are librarians.

- **The object of the game is to put the books in the appropriate places in the library.**

- They should take it in turns to take a book and place it where they think it belongs on the 'shelves' in the LIBRARY PLAN.

- They can check if they were right by turning the books over to see the subject on the back.

GAME 2 Personalising
pairwork discussion
- If students are still at school, get them to draw a plan of their timetable. If not, give them a copy of the imaginary TIMETABLE or draw it on the board.

- Put students in pairs and ask them to discuss their timetable:

  Which subjects do/did they like?
  What is/was their favourite?
  What is/was their least favourite?
  What is/was their favourite/least favourite day?

GAME 3 Communicating [Long game]
whole class search game
Freshers' week
- Give each student a copy of the HALL OF RESIDENCE PLAN and a REGISTRATION FORM.

- Ask them to look at the plan and work out which is their room.

- Get them to write their name on the door.

- **The object of the game is to find out who lives in all the other rooms.**

- To do this they will have to get up and go round the room asking other people what their name is and what they study, and write the names on the appropriate doors, e.g. *'What's your name? What subject are you studying?'*

- No one is allowed to tell other students which room they live in!

- Get students to sit down as they finish and check their answers with the person next to them.

---

8 Sports

Topic area
sport

Vocabulary focus
sports: *football, tennis, golf, skiing, athletics, hockey, ice hockey, badminton, baseball, cricket*

equipment: *shuttlecock, hockey stick, bat, ball, skates, skis, running shoes, racquet, golf club, net, goal, cap, pole, boots, stumps*

places: *slopes, court, pitch, golf course, track, rink, diamond*

people: *team, players, competitors, opponent, referee, umpire*

events: *match, round, tournament, championship, cup*

Structures

there are (eleven players in a team), you need (a shuttlecock to play badminton), (tennis) is played on a (court)

Materials and preparation

GAME 1 Copy and cut up one set of SPORTS WORDS per pair of students; also one set of ADDITIONAL WORDS and one set of SPORTS PICTURES per group of four students.

GAME 2 None.

GAME 3 Copy and cut up one set of QUIZ questions for each group of 6–8 students.

How to use the games

GAME 1 Memorising

1 pairwork sorting game

- Divide the class into pairs.

- Give each pair a set of SPORTS WORDS.

- Ask them to place the cards face up on the table.

- **The object of the game is to sort the cards out into four piles: *equipment*, *places*, *people* and *events*.**

- The pair that finish first (with all correct) are the winners.

2 small group collecting game

- Ask the pairs to join up with another pair to make groups of four.

- Ask them to put aside one set of their cards.

- From the remaining set of SPORTS WORDS cards, ask them to discard the *people* and *events* cards, keeping *equipment* and *places*.

- Give each group a set of ADDITIONAL WORDS and a set of SPORTS PICTURES cards.

- They should place the 10 sports picture cards face down in a pile in the middle of the table.

- They should add the additional words to the pile of sports words (making 40 cards), shuffle them and deal them out to each player.

- Player 1 should take the top card from the pile of sports pictures.

- Without showing it to the others, he should call out the name of the sport: e.g. *'Football.'*

- **The object of the game is to match sports with the appropriate picture of equipment and places needed for playing the sport.**

- The other players should look at the cards in their hands to see if they have any word cards that match that sport.

- For each sport there are three equipment cards and one place card: e.g. for football: *ball, boots, goal, pitch*; for tennis: *ball, net, racquet, court*.

- The players who say the correct words first, producing the appropriate cards, may discard their cards.

- Then it is the next player's turn to take a card from the pile and call out the sport.

- The player who gets rid of her cards first is the winner.

ANSWERS: football: ball, goal, boots, pitch; **golf:** ball, golf club, tee, golf course; **athletics:** running shoes, hurdle, pole, track; **badminton:** shuttlecock, net, racquet, court; **cricket:** ball, bat, stumps, pitch; **tennis:** ball, net, racquet, court; **skiing:** skis, sticks, boots, slopes; **hockey:** hockey stick, ball, goal, field; **baseball:** ball, bat, cap, diamond; **ice hockey:** stick, skates, goal, rink

GAME 2 Personalising

pairwork guessing game

- Ask students to choose (silently) their favourite sport and write a description of it:

  How many players are needed?
  What equipment is needed?
  Where is it played?
  Why do I like it?

- Put students in pairs and get them to read each other their descriptions without saying the name of the sport – can their partner guess the sport?

GAME 3 Communicating

small group quiz game

Sports quiz

- Put students in groups of 6–8 and get them to organise themselves in two teams of 3–4 and give their team a name.

- Give each group a set of QUIZ cards.

- Ask them to put these face down in the middle of the table.

- Team 1 should turn up the first card and ask Team 2 the question.

- If Team 2 answers correctly they can keep the card.

- If they cannot answer or answer incorrectly, Team 1 keep the card.

- Then it is Team 2's turn to turn up a card.

- **The object of the game is to win the most cards.**

9 Tools and DIY

Topic area
tools

Vocabulary focus
nail, screw, Rawlplug, nut, bracket, paintbrush, hammer, chisel, spanner, screwdriver, vice, drill, saw, spirit level, plane, pliers, mallet, sandpaper, tyre levers, wheel brace, jack

Structures
I need ..., have you got ... ?

Materials and preparation

GAME 1 Copy and cut up one set of TOOLS WORDS and one set of TOOLS PICTURES for each pair of students.

GAME 2 None.

GAME 3 Copy one HOUSEHOLD JOBS sheet and one TOOLS PICTURES sheet for every four students. Cut up the cards, keeping the numbered household jobs separate from the same-numbered row of pictures.

How to use the games

GAME 1 Memorising
pairwork matching game

- Divide students into pairs.

- Give each pair a set of TOOLS PICTURES cards and a set of TOOLS WORDS cards.

- Ask them to mix the two sets up and spread them out face down on the table.

- They should take it in turns to turn up a card and lay it flat on the table.

- **The object of the game is to match words with the corresponding pictures.**

- When a card is turned up that corresponds to a picture or a word that is already face up on the table, the first person to say the name of the tool and take both cards may keep the cards.

- The student with most cards at the end is the winner.

GAME 2 Personalising
pairwork discussion

- Ask students to work in pairs and spread the TOOLS PICTURES cards out on the table in front of them.

- Ask them to think of three jobs that need doing at home.

- Ask them to make a list of the tools they would need to do that job.

- Get them to compare their answers.

GAME 3 Communicating
whole class exchanging and collecting game
Mr Fixit

- Give each student a HOUSEHOLD JOBS card.

- Tell them these are jobs that need doing at home.

- Then give each student any four TOOLS PICTURES cards that don't correspond to the jobs on the student's card.

- **The object of the game is to get the right tools for the jobs.**

- To do this the students will need to move around the class asking others for the tools they need, e.g. '*I need a hammer. Have you got one?*'

- Ask them to sit down when they have got the tools they need and have given away the ones they originally had.

10 Office objects

Topic area
stationery and office objects

Vocabulary focus
computer, printer, photocopier, filing cabinet, files, telephone, fax machine, desk, desk lamp, calculator, diary, calendar, in-tray, out-tray, swivel chair, wastepaper bin, paperclip, stapler, hole punch, memo pad, mouse mat, telephone directories, mobile phone, stationery cupboard, answering machine

Structures
where's the … ?, it's + place prepositions, would

Materials and preparation

GAME 1 Copy one OFFICE PICTURE and one set of LABELS per group of 3–4. Cut up the LABELS. Keep the ANSWERS back until students have finished the game.

GAME 2 One set of LABELS per pair.

GAME 3 One set of UNTIDY OFFICE pictures (A and B) per pair.

How to use the games

GAME 1 Memorising
small group matching game

- Divide students into groups of 3–4.

- Give each group an OFFICE PICTURE and a set of LABELS.

- They should put the picture where they can all see it and the labels face down in a pile on the table.

- Then they take it in turns to pick up a label from the pile and say the word(s).

- The first person to say the number (on the picture) that corresponds to the item on the label can keep the label. He should write the number on the label.

- **The object of the game is to match all the words with the numbers on the picture.**

- At the end they can check their numbered labels against the ANSWERS sheet.

- The person with most labels (correctly numbered) is the winner.

GAME 2 Personalising
pairwork draw and describe

- Ask students to spread the LABELS out on the table and look at them.

- Ask them to design their ideal office:

  What would they include?
  Where would they put the objects?

- Ask them to make a labelled drawing or plan.

- Then group them in pairs and ask them to explain their plan to their partner.

GAME 3 Communicating
pairwork information gap game
Untidy offices
- Divide students into pairs and give one student the UNTIDY OFFICE picture A and the other student picture B.

- The large picture shows their office. The small pictures show things they can't find.

- They should ask their partner where their lost objects are, e.g. *'Where's the paperclip?'*

- The other student looks at her picture and replies, e.g. *'It's beside the out-tray.'*

- **The object of the game is to find out from the other player where the things are and to draw them in on their office picture.**

11 Computers

Topic area
computers and computing

Vocabulary focus
hardware: *screen, monitor, VDU, keyboard, mouse, printer, scanner, laptop, disks, hard disk, floppy disk, CD-ROM drive, cable, modem*

software (etc): *Internet, web site/website, World Wide Web, word processing, spreadsheet, database, graphics, e-mail/email, program*

commands: *icons, open, close, save, print, cut, copy, paste, clear, find, insert table*

actions: *click (a mouse), pull down (a menu), download (information), visit (a web site), scan in (a document), print out (a file), install (a program), scroll down (a page)*

Extra vocabulary
display, grid, manipulation, network, text, sound, links, published, coded, cursor, Escape, system, error, brightness, control, connected, damaged, surfing, double-click, Recycle Bin, desktop, select, Restore, expert, switch on

Structures
simple present, *can, won't, may*, imperatives, passives, conditions *(if ... then ...)*

Materials and preparation

GAME 1 Decide which set(s) of words you want your students to practise. Then follow the instructions below. For each pair of students:

For *hardware*: Copy the HARDWARE picture and a set of HARDWARE WORDS and SOFTWARE WORDS (not the SOFTWARE DEFINITIONS). Cut up the words.

For *software*: Copy and cut up one set of SOFTWARE WORDS and SOFTWARE DEFINITIONS.

For *commands*: Copy and cut up one set of ICONS AND COMMANDS, separating the words from the pictures.

For *actions*: Copy and cut up one set of COLLOCATION cards.

GAME 2 Copy one QUESTIONNAIRE for each student.

GAME 3 Copy and cut up one complete set of TROUBLESHOOTING cards for each group of 6–8 students.

How to use the games
GAME 1 Memorising
Divide students into pairs. Depending on which set(s) of words you are practising, follow the instructions below:

1 pairwork labelling game: *Hardware*
- Give each pair the HARDWARE and SOFTWARE WORDS cards.

- Ask them to divide the cards into two groups: *hardware* and *software*.

- Then give them the picture.

- Ask them to put the hardware words as labels in the right place on the picture.

  ANSWERS: **a** screen **b** monitor/VDU **c** keyboard **d** mouse **e** printer **f** scanner **g** laptop **h** hard disk **i** floppy disk **j** CD-ROM drive **k** cable **l** modem

2 pairwork matching game: *Software*
- Give each pair the SOFTWARE WORDS and DEFINITIONS cards.

- They should spread these out face down on the table and take it in turns to turn them up one at a time.

- **The object of the game is to match words and definitions.**

- When a word or definition is turned up that matches one that is already face up, the first person to pick up the pair can keep the cards.

- The person with most cards at the end is the winner.

  ANSWERS: **1** word processing **2** spreadsheet **3** database **4** graphics **5** e-mail **6** Internet **7** World Wide Web **8** web site **9** program

3 pairwork matching game: *Commands*
- Give each pair the ICONS AND COMMANDS cards (words and pictures, cut apart).

- They should spread the commands on the table, face up, and put the icons in a pile, face down.

- They take it in turns to turn up the icon cards one at a time.

- **The object of the game is to match icons and commands.**

- When an icon is turned up, the first person to say the appropriate command can keep both cards.

- The person with most cards at the end is the winner.

4 small group matching game: *Actions*

- Give each pair a set of COLLOCATION cards.

- Ask them to play in groups of four, in competition with another pair.

- Each pair should spread their own set of cards out on the table and look at them.

- **The object of the game is to match all verbs and nouns.**

- The pair who can do this fastest (correctly) are the winners.

GAME 2 Personalising
pairwork questionnaire and discussion

- Give each student a copy of the QUESTIONNAIRE.

- They should fill this in for themselves and then compare answers with another student.

GAME 3 Communicating
small group matching game | RULES SHEET |
Troubleshooting

- Divide students into groups of 3–4.

- Give each group a complete set of TROUBLESHOOTING cards, keeping Problems separate from Solutions.

- Ask them to deal them out, each category equally, to all players.

- **The object of the game is to find the solutions to your problems.**

- To do this, the first player should select a problem from his hand and tell the others about it (without mentioning the number on the card).

- The player with appropriate advice should offer it.

- They can check if the advice was correct by comparing the numbers on the cards.

- If it was correct, the player who gave the advice can keep the cards.

- If not, another player can offer advice.

- At the end, the player with most pairs of cards is the winner.

12 Actions (1)

Topic area
human actions

Vocabulary focus
waving, holding, pressing, grinning, shouting, whispering, tripping, rushing, arguing, hopping, chatting, hugging, twisting, grabbing, stealing, pointing, yawning, hitting, shaking, tugging, smiling, giving

Extra vocabulary
have a good chat, shake hands

Structures
present continuous, simple past, *because ...* , *the last time I ... was ...*

Materials and preparation

GAME 1 Copy and cut up one set of ACTIONS cards for each pair of students.

GAME 2 Copy one QUESTIONNAIRE for each student.

GAME 3 Copy one set of STREET SCENE pictures (A and B) for each pair of students.

How to use the games

GAME 1 Memorising
1 pairwork sorting game

- Divide your class into pairs.

- Give each pair a set of ACTIONS cards.

- Get them to divide the cards into sets: *legs*, *hands* and *mouth*, according to the part of the body that is most involved in the action.

2 small group guessing game

- Then get each pair to join up with another pair.

- They should use one set of ACTIONS cards only and put them in a pile face down in the middle of the table.

- Each player should take it in turns to take a card and mime the action on it to the rest of the group.

- **The object of the game is to guess the mimed actions.**

- The player who guesses first can keep the card.

- The player with most cards at the end is the winner.

GAME 2 Personalising
pairwork questionnaire and discussion

- Give out a copy of the QUESTIONNAIRE to each student in the class.

- Ask them to fill it in individually.

- Then put students in pairs to compare answers, e.g. *'I yawned this morning because I woke up too early.' 'The last time I smiled was this morning – at a little baby in the bus queue.'*

GAME 3 Communicating
pairwork information gap game
Street life

- Divide your class into pairs.

- Give one student in each pair STREET SCENE picture A and the other student picture B.

- They should not show their pictures to each other.

- There are six differences between the pictures.

- **The object of the game is to find the six differences.**

- To do this they will have to describe what is happening in their pictures to each other and note down the differences as they find them: e.g. *'In picture A a girl is yawning. In picture B she is smiling.'*

13 Actions (2)

Topic area
ways of performing actions

Vocabulary focus
quietly, loudly, sadly, happily, slowly, quickly, angrily, calmly, impatiently, patiently, carefully, carelessly, aggressively, gently, timidly, bravely, joyfully, gloomily, nervously, confidently

Extra vocabulary
real, imaginary, shut, door, baby room, sing, bath, tell, open, present, late bus, run, carry, trifle, talk, bump, car, crash, crying, talk, hurry, write, dentist, waiting room, teach, tiger, rucksack, uphill, walk, letter, read, delayed, snake, pick up, envelope, exam results, view

Structures
adverbs, simple past, *how would you … ?, I would …*

Materials and preparation

GAME 1 Copy and cut up one set of ADVERBS cards for each pair of students.

GAME 2 Copy one QUESTIONNAIRE for each student.

GAME 3 Copy and cut up one set of GENTLY DOES IT cards and one set of ADVERBS cards for each group of 3–4 students.

How to use the games

GAME 1 Memorising
pairwork matching game

- Divide your class into pairs.

- Give each pair a set of ADVERBS cards.

- Get them to spread them out on the table, face down.

- They should take it in turns to turn up a card one at a time (and leave it turned up).

- **The object of the game is to match opposites.**

- When a player spots two opposites she says the words and may collect the cards and keep them.

- In some cases there is more than one possibility (e.g. *sadly* or *gloomily* can match with either *happily* or *joyfully*).

- The person with most cards at the end of the game is the winner.

GAME 2 Personalising
pairwork questionnaire and discussion

- Give out a QUESTIONNAIRE to each student.

- Ask them to fill it in by themselves.

- Then ask them to work with a partner and compare their answers.

- The partner's task is to decide which sentences are real and which are imaginary.

GAME 3 Communicating
small group matching game   [RULES SHEET]
Gently does it

- Divide your class into groups of 3–4.

- Give out a set of GENTLY DOES IT cards and a set of ADVERBS cards to each group.

- They should shuffle and deal out each pack separately, so that players hold both sorts of cards.

- The first player should select one of the picture cards and ask a question about it, beginning 'How would you … ?' (e.g. 'How would you shut the door of the baby's room?') They don't have to use the prompt phrases.

- Players should try to give an appropriate answer, producing one of the adverbs cards in their hand, e.g. 'Quietly!' or 'Gently!'

- If the other players feel the answer is not appropriate they may dispute it, or offer their own suggestions. The player who asked the question can decide which answer is best.

- When a match has been found, both players can discard the matching cards.

- **The object of the game is to get rid of all your cards.**

- The player who does this first is the winner.

NOTE: As there are different possibilities for answers to some of the questions, depending on how the game turns out, some players may find that as the game progresses there are fewer immediately obvious answers for some of the questions. They will have to become more ingenious in arguing the case for some of their answers (e.g. arguing that they are waiting at the dentist's angrily, because he pulled the wrong tooth out). The rule still applies: the questioner decides on the most appropriate or best explanation!

14 Approval and disapproval

Topic area
adjectives for approval and disapproval

Vocabulary focus
positive: *good, nice, brilliant, fantastic, wonderful, amazing, great, terrific, sweet, cute, super, lovely, marvellous, excellent*

neutral: *okay, all right/alright, not bad, so-so*

negative: *awful, terrible, horrible, disgusting, dreadful, ridiculous, vile, nasty, boring, horrific*

Extra vocabulary
Students may request vocabulary for Games 2 and 3, e.g. professions, objects, etc.

Structures
... *is/are* (adjective), *I think that* (noun) *is* (adjective), *what do you think of ...* , *are you thinking of ...*

Materials and preparation

GAME 1 Copy and cut up one set of ADJECTIVES cards for each pair of students.

GAME 2 One set of ADJECTIVES cards for each pair of students.

GAME 3 One set of ADJECTIVES cards for each group of 3–4 students.

How to use the games

GAME 1 Memorising
pairwork sorting and ordering game

- Divide students into pairs and give each pair a set of ADJECTIVES cards.

- Ask them to lay them out on the table, face up.

- **The object of the game is to sort the cards into three groups: *positive*, *neutral* and *negative*.**

- Students should work together to do this.

- When they have finished they should turn the cards face down and try to remember the words in each group.

GAME 2 Personalising
pairwork discussion

- Ask each pair of students to shuffle their set of cards and divide them equally between them.

- Ask them to think of something about their own country (or Britain if you prefer) to be described by each of their cards. Give a few examples (e.g. for Britain: *the weather is dreadful, the beer is great, the transport is terrible, the food is all right.*)

- When they have finished, they can compare notes and see if they agree.

GAME 3 Communicating
small group guessing game   RULES SHEET
Strong feelings

- Ask pairs of students to join with another to form groups of 3–4.

- Each group needs one set of ADJECTIVES cards.

- They should place these in a pile in the middle of the table, face down.

- The first student should take a card and silently read the adjective, without showing the word to anyone.

- He should think of a person, object or place about which he has that opinion, and mime a clue for the others.

- **The object of the game is for the others to guess who or what he is thinking of, and his opinion of it.**

- They can do this by asking questions, e.g. *'An actress – are you thinking of an actress?' 'No.' 'A singer then?' 'Yes.' 'Madonna?' 'Yes.' 'You think Madonna is great?' 'NO!' 'Oh, right, you think she's awful?'*, etc.

- Player 1 may answer only 'Yes' or 'No'.

15 People

Topic area
people's appearance

Vocabulary focus
general appearance: (height:) *short, small, tall, medium height*; (build:) *overweight, tubby, plump/plumpish, well built, medium build, skinny, slim, thin, muscular*; (beauty:) *beautiful, attractive, pretty, handsome, good-looking, plain, ugly*; (dress:) *smartly / well / elegantly / casually / scruffily / neatly dressed*; (mood:) *anxious- / happy- / angry- / sad- / tired-looking*

face and head: (hair type:) *bald, short / long / wavy / curly / straight hair*; (hair colour:) *blonde / red / auburn / grey / white / fair / black / brown / mousy / dark hair*; (nose:) *long / hooked / broad / snub nose*; (lips:) *full / thick / thin lips*; (eyes:) *round / slanting / almond eyes*; (chin:) *pointed / double chin*; (face shape:) *square / round / oval / heart-shaped / long face*

Extra vocabulary
marriage bureau, (dream) romance, (available/ideal) partner

Structures
has/have (got), compound adjectives: *blue-eyed, round-faced*, etc.

Materials and preparation

GAME 1 Decide which set of vocabulary you want to practise: *general appearance* or *face and head*.

For *general appearance*: Copy and cut up one set of APPEARANCE words and one set of APPEARANCE pictures per group of 3–4.

For *face and head*: Copy and cut up one set of FACE AND HEAD words and one set of FACE AND HEAD pictures per group of 3–4.

GAME 2 None.

GAME 3 Copy and cut up one set of DREAM ROMANCE cards and one set of AVAILABLE PARTNERS cards for two thirds of the total number of students.

How to use the games

GAME 1 Memorising
1 small group collecting game: *Appearance*
- Divide your class into groups of 3–4.

- Give each group a set of APPEARANCE picture cards. Students should take one card each.

- Give them a set of APPEARANCE words. They should spread these out face down on the table.

- They should take it in turns to pick up one word card and read it out.

- If a player thinks the word describes her picture, she may claim it.

- **The object of the game is to get five words that describe your picture.**

- The player who does this first is the winner.

2 small group sorting game: *Face and head*

- Divide students into groups of 3–4.

- Give each group a set of FACE AND HEAD words. They should spread these face down on the table.

- Then give each group a set of FACE AND HEAD pictures. Students take one picture card each.

- Then they play the game in exactly the same way as above.

- **The object of the game is to get at least six words that describe your picture: one word each for *hair*, *face*, *nose*, *eyes*, *lips* and *chin*.**

GAME 2 Personalising
pairwork guessing game

- Ask students to write a description of one member of their family.

- Get them to read it to a partner, without saying who the relative is.

- Their partner has to guess who it is.

GAME 3 Communicating
whole class matching game
Datelines

- Divide your class into one third and two thirds.

- Divide the one third into three groups and get each group to sit behind a desk in different areas of the room.

- Tell them they are Marriage Bureaux. (They can invent names for themselves if they like, and make a sign.)

- Give each bureau a selection of AVAILABLE PARTNERS cards.

- Tell the remaining students they are looking for partners. Give them a DREAM ROMANCE card each.

- **The object of the game is to find a partner at one of the marriage bureaux.**

- To do this they will have to visit the marriage bureaux, describing what they have in mind (the picture on their card).

- They should not show their cards to the marriage bureaux and the marriage bureaux should not show their cards to the clients.

- When they have described their ideal partner the marriage bureau may look through their cards to see if they have anything that vaguely corresponds. They describe this card to the client.

- If the client is satisfied, he can take the card. If he thinks he can do better he can try another bureau.

WARNING: They may have to settle for less than their ideal.

16 Colours and shapes

Topic area
colours, shapes and forms

Vocabulary focus
colours: *khaki, mauve, fawn/beige, turquoise, cream, crimson, scarlet, navy, off-white, yellowy-green, reddish-brown*

shapes: (flat:) *oval, square, (semi-)circular, rectangular, triangular, hexagonal, octagonal, diamond-shaped, heart-shaped*; (solid:) *cylindrical, spiral, (hemi-)spherical, cube/cuboid, conical, pyramid- / dome- / egg- / wedge-shaped*

forms: *hollow, solid, sharp, blunt, pointed, rounded, concave, convex, straight, bent, crooked, curved, smooth, rough, jagged*

Extra vocabulary
materials (*metal, cloth, plastic*), items of clothing, parts of the body, more usual colour names (*red, brown, green, purple*, etc.)

Structures
be, have, place prepositions, *it's used for + -ing*

Materials and preparation

GAME 1 Decide which set of adjectives you want to practise.

For *colours*: Copy and cut up one set of COLOURS cards for each group of 3–4 students. Bring into the class eleven objects, one for each of the colours on the cards, e.g. various items of clothing, books, pencils, flowers, fruit and vegetables. If you can't find an object for a particular colour, draw a picture using coloured pencils or paint.

For *shapes*: Copy and cut up one set of SHAPES WORDS and one set of SHAPES PICTURES cards for each pair of students.

For *forms*: Copy and cut up one set of OPPOSITE FORMS cards for each pair of students.

GAME 2
1. Copy and cut up one set of COLOURS cards for each pair of students.

2. None.

GAME 3 Copy and cut up one set of PLANET ZARG and PLANET THARG cards for each group of 4–6 students.

How to use the games

GAME 1 Memorising

1 small group matching game: *Colours*

- Divide your class into groups of 3–4.

- Give each group a set of COLOURS cards.

- Place the objects at the front of the room where everyone can see them.

- Make sure they know the names of the objects. (Write them on the board or label each object if they are unfamiliar words.)

- Ask the groups to place the cards face down on the table and to take it in turns to turn them up one at a time.

- **The object of the game is to match the colour on the card with one of the objects at the front.**

- The first player to say the name of the correct object when the card is turned up may keep the card.

- The player with most cards at the end is the winner.

2 pairwork sorting and matching game: *Shapes*

- Divide your class into pairs.

- Give each pair a set of SHAPES WORDS cards and a set of SHAPES PICTURES cards.

- Ask them to take the words first and to sort them into two groups: *flat* and *solid* (i.e. two-dimensional and three-dimensional) shapes.

- Then ask them to shuffle both packs together and to spread out all the cards face down on the table.

- They should take it in turns to turn up the cards one at a time.

- **The object of the game is to match words and pictures.**

- When a player can match the card she is turning up with one that has already been turned up, she may keep the cards.

- The player with most cards at the end is the winner.

3 pairwork matching and collecting game: *Forms*

- Divide your class into pairs.

- Give each pair a set of OPPOSITE FORMS cards.

- Get them to begin by spreading all the cards out face up and matching the pairs of opposites. (*Straight* is the opposite of *bent*, *crooked* and *curved*; *smooth* is the opposite of both *rough* and *jagged*.)

- They should then shuffle the cards and deal themselves five cards each and put the rest face down in a pile in the middle of the table. They may look at their cards.

- **The object of the game is to collect matching pairs of opposites.**

- If they have any cards in their hand that match already (e.g. *sharp*, *blunt*), they may put these down as a 'trick'.

- Then Player 1 begins by asking his partner for a card that will match one of those he holds, e.g. *'Have you got "smooth"?'*

- If Player 2 has the card, she must give it to Player 1, who can lay both cards down as a trick.

- If not, Player 1 must take a card from the pile.

- Then it is Player 2's turn.

- The player with most tricks at the end is the winner.

GAME 2 Personalising

1 pairwork discussion game

- Divide students into pairs.

- Give each pair a set of COLOURS cards.

- Get them to put these in a pile face down on the table.

- They should take it in turns to turn up one card at a time and lay it face up in front of them.

- They should tell each other what the colour makes them think of, e.g. *'Scarlet makes me think of English postboxes'* or *'It makes me think of my daughter's coat'*.

2 pairwork guessing game

- Get students to close their eyes and think of an object they have at home that is precious to them in some way.

- Then put them in pairs.

- They should describe the object without saying what it is.

- Their partner must guess.

GAME 3 Communicating

small group information gap game
Return from the Forbidden Planet

- Divide your class into groups of 4–6. Each group should then form two teams of 2–3.

- Tell one team in each group they are astronauts who have returned from a mission to Planet Zarg. They did not see any inhabitants but found evidence of intelligent life. They are radioing back to Mission Control to describe their findings.

- Give this team the PLANET ZARG card.

- The other team in each group is Mission Control; they will need pen and paper.

- The astronauts should describe the objects on their card to Mission Control without saying what the objects are.

- Mission Control should try to draw the objects and work out what they are used for.

- **The object of the game is to work out what the inhabitants of Planet Zarg look like.**

- When they have heard all the descriptions of the objects, Mission Control should work together to try and draw a picture of what they think the inhabitants look like.

- When they have finished, tell the teams to reverse roles. Give the previous Mission Control the PLANET THARG card.

17 Scenery

Topic area
landscape and countryside

Vocabulary focus
landscapes: *farmland, desert, jungle / rain forest, forest, woodland, hills, grassland, pasture, moorland, mountain range, swamp, canyon, bush*

terrains: *flat, level, rolling, sloping, mountainous, steep, rich, lush, densely, thickly, sparsely, craggy, rocky, marshy, wild, bare, barren*

atmospheres: *mysterious, exciting, desolate, gentle, dramatic, majestic, gloomy, lonely, peaceful, monotonous, awe-inspiring, romantic*

Extra vocabulary
landscape, meadows, countryside, plain, hilly, grassy, dotted, tangled, steamy

animal names (provided on the cards): *cow, camel, monkey, squirrel, sheep, goat, horse, rabbit, alligator, lizard, lion, chamois, parrot, racoon, antelope, frog*

Structures
There is/are …

Materials and preparation

GAME 1 Decide which set(s) of vocabulary you want to practise: *landscapes, terrains* or *atmospheres*.

For *landscapes*: Copy and cut up one set of LANDSCAPES WORDS cards and one set of LANDSCAPES PICTURES cards per pair of students and one set of WILDLIFE cards per group of 3–4.

For *terrains*: Copy and cut up one set of LANDSCAPES PICTURES cards and one set of TERRAINS cards per pair of students.

For *atmospheres*: Copy and cut up two sets of LANDSCAPES PICTURES and three sets of ATMOSPHERES cards per group of 3–4.

GAME 2 None.

GAME 3 Copy enough of the LANDSCAPES PICTURES for each pair of students to have five pictures. Cut them up and put them in a bag.

How to use the games

GAME 1 Memorising
Decide which set(s) of vocabulary items you want to practise.

1 pairwork matching game: *Landscapes*
- Divide your class into pairs.

- Give each pair one set of LANDSCAPES PICTURES and one set of LANDSCAPES WORDS.

- Get them to lay out the pictures face up and put the word cards in a pile on the table, face down.

- They should take it in turns to turn the word cards up one at a time.

- **The object of the game is to match words and pictures.**

- When they have done this they should divide them into two groups: *Landscapes we can see in our/my country* and *Landscapes abroad*.

- (If the students come from the same country this can obviously be done cooperatively; if they come from different countries they will have to do this one at a time and compare their answers.)

- Finally ask pairs to join with another pair and give them a set of WILDLIFE cards.

- They should put these in a pile on the table, face down.

- They should put away the landscape word cards and deal out the landscape picture cards.

- Get them to turn up the first wildlife card. The player who has an appropriate landscape habitat for that animal can call out the name of the landscape (e.g. *farmland, desert, forest*) and produce the card. There is more than one possibility for some animals.

- The first player to produce an appropriate landscape habitat can keep the pair of cards.

- The player with most cards at the end is the winner.

2 pairwork matching game: *Terrains*
- Divide your class into pairs.

- Give each pair a set of LANDSCAPES PICTURES and a set of TERRAINS cards.

- They should spread out the landscape cards face up on the table and put the terrain cards face down in a pile.

- The first player should turn up a terrain card from the pile and read it out.

- The object of the game is to match terrain descriptions with landscapes.

- The first person to match the terrain description with a picture it describes, repeating the phrase, can collect the pair of cards.

3 small group matching game: *Atmospheres*
- Divide students into groups of 3–4.

- Give each group two sets of LANDSCAPES PICTURES and three sets of ATMOSPHERES cards.

- They should put the landscape pictures face down in a pile in the middle of the table and deal out the atmosphere cards.

- Player 1 turns up a picture from the pile.

- **The object of the game is to match landscapes with atmosphere adjectives.**

- The first player to call out one of the adjectives in his hand that correctly describes the picture can collect the two cards.

- Player 2 turns up the next picture card.

- There is more than one possibility for each picture.

- Some suggestions may be open to dispute: e.g. it would be difficult to describe the moorland or the canyon as 'gentle', but people may see the forest as 'mysterious', 'peaceful' or 'gloomy' according to temperament. The rest of the group should decide whether the adjective is appropriate and in cases of dispute the teacher should act as arbiter.

GAME 2 Personalising
pairwork visualisation

- Get students to close their eyes and imagine:

  a hot, steamy swamp
  the top of a mountain range
  a bare, lonely desert
  a rich landscape of rolling hills and meadow
  wild moorland
  a peaceful woodland
  a gloomy forest

- Conjure up each scene for them, describing a few details slowly as they listen with their eyes closed, e.g. *'Imagine a hot, steamy swamp. Imagine you are there. Why are you there – what are you doing? What can you see? How do you feel?'*

- When you have finished each scene, they should open their eyes and discuss with a partner what they were doing in each place and why.

GAME 3 Communicating   `Long game`
pairwork arranging game
Dreamscapes

- Divide your class into pairs.

- Pass round the bag of LANDSCAPES PICTURES cards and get each pair to take five cards.

- Ask them to spread the cards out on the table (randomly, not in a straight line) and look at them.

- Tell them these images all come from the same dream.

- Get each student to imagine a dream: Where was the first scene of their dream? What were they doing there? What happened next? Where did the next action take place?

- The images can be in any order in their dream.

- Get them to write their dream down, describing the landscapes as well as recounting the actions.

- If you think the students need extra support, you can put the landscape, terrain and atmosphere words on the board to remind them.

- When they have finished, one student should tell her dream to her partner.

- **The object of the game is for the partner to arrange the pictures in the order described in the dream.**

- As each student listens to his partner's dream, he should arrange the pictures in the order of the dream sequence.

18 Sounds

Topic area
sounds and noises

Vocabulary focus
whistle, bang, click, thump, hum, howl, cry, rumble, scream, roar, growl, tick, chirp, pop, rattle, rustle, squeak, creak, buzz, splash

Extra vocabulary
noise, bump, clang, yowl, groan, moan, mumble, grumble, drop, plop, snore, crash, hammer, nail, castanets, boots, fridge, wolf, baby, train, ghost, lion, dog, time bomb, bird, tree, champagne cork, rattle, breeze, leaves, door, burglar, floorboard, bee, tap, sink, overflow

Structures
I can hear something + -ing, I can hear a + -ing noise, simple present, present continuous

---

Materials and preparation

GAME 1 Copy and cut up one set of NOISES cards for each pair of students.

GAME 2 None.

GAME 3 Copy and cut up two sets of SOUNDS PICTURES cards for each group of 3–4.

How to use the games
GAME 1 Memorising
1 pairwork guessing game

- Divide students into pairs.

- Give each pair a set of the NOISES cards.

- Get them to put these in a pile face down in the middle of the table.

- They should take it in turns to turn up a card and make the noise written on the card.

- **The object of the game is to name the noise the other person is making.**

2 small group guessing game

- When students have played the first game, join the pairs up to make groups of four.

- They should put away one pack of the noises cards and place the other pack in a pile face down in the middle of the table.

- They should take it in turns to take a card from the pile and give the others a clue about the sound, e.g. *'Clocks make this sound'* or *'Lions make this noise'*.

- **The object of the game is to guess the noise.**

- The first player who guesses correctly may keep the card.

- The player with most cards at the end is the winner.

GAME 2 Personalising
pairwork visualisation and guessing game

- Ask students to close their eyes. What sounds can they hear around them?

- Then write these phrases on the board:
  at home in the kitchen
  in the middle of a wood
  on a busy road
  in the jungle
  in a city street

- Ask students to imagine what sounds they could hear in these places and to write a list of sounds for each place.

- Then put them in pairs and get them to read each other their lists without saying the name of the place.

- Their partner has to guess where they are.

VARIATION: A number of sounds have rhyming names, e.g. thump/bump, bang/clang, tick/click, growl/howl/yowl, groan/moan, mumble/rumble/grumble, squeak/creak, drop/pop/plop, roar/snore, splash/crash.

If you think your class would like it, you could introduce these extra words, then get them to choose a place or event and make a rhyming poem using these words, e.g.

NIGHT IN THE JUNGLE
Squeak
Creak
Howl
Yowl
Growl
Roar …
Snore

Students read out their 'poems' and the rest of the class guess what's happening!

GAME 3 Communicating
small group guessing game `RULES SHEET`
Sound pictures

- Divide your class into groups of 3–4.

- Give two sets of SOUNDS PICTURES cards to each group.

- They should shuffle the two sets together into one pack and deal these out equally to all players.

- The players may look at their cards but shouldn't show them to the others.

- If they have two that match they can put them down as a 'trick'.

- The first player should select a card from her hand, describe what she can 'hear' and ask the others to guess what it is, e.g. (selecting the picture of a wolf) *'I can hear something howling. What is it?'* or (selecting the picture of a baby) *'I can hear a rattling noise. Do you know what it is?'*

- The player with the matching card should answer: *'Don't be scared, it's only a wolf!'* or *'It's okay, it's only the baby shaking his rattle'* and give her the card.

- The first player can then put down both cards as a trick.

- **The object of the game is to give accurate clues to the sound pictures, and collect the most cards.**

19 Sensations

Topic area
adjectives for touch, taste and smell

Vocabulary focus
light, heavy, wet, dry, cold, hot, rough, smooth, hard, soft, prickly, furry, slippery, slimy, greasy, hairy, sweet, sour, bitter, salty, spicy, bland/tasteless, fragrant, foul-smelling

Structures
be, have got, simple present, sense verbs + adjective (*it feels/tastes/smells …*)

Materials and preparation
GAME 1 Copy and cut up one set of OBJECTS (1) cards per pair of students. Don't forget the words on the back.

GAME 2 One set of OBJECTS (1) word cards per pair.

GAME 3 Copy and cut up one set of OBJECTS (1) cards without the words on the back, and one set of OBJECTS (2) cards, for each group of 3–4 students.

How to use the games
GAME 1 Memorising
pairwork guessing game

- Divide students into pairs and give each pair a set of OBJECTS (1) cards.

- Ask them to put them in a pile on the table, word-side up.

- They should take the cards one at a time and try to guess what picture is on the reverse side.

- When both have had a guess, they can turn the card over and see if either was right.

- Then ask them to spread the cards out picture-side up.

- One student should think of a card, without telling the other which it is.

- He should try to remember the adjective associated with it and tell his partner something about the object, e.g. *'It's light'* or *'It feels slippery'*.

- **The object of the game is for the partner to guess which card the first student is thinking of.**

- The partner may ask questions, e.g. *'Does it feel soft?'* *'Is it hard?'*

- When the partner has guessed correctly, then it is her turn to choose a card, and so on.

GAME 2 Personalising
pairwork discussion
- Ask students to think of objects and food items in their kitchen at home.
- Can they find one for each adjective? Give them a set of OBJECTS (1) word cards to remember the adjectives, or write them up on the board. Circulate to supply vocabulary.
- Then put them in pairs to compare lists.

GAME 3 Communicating
small group matching game   RULES SHEET
Sensation snap
- Put students in groups of 3–4.
- Give each group a set of OBJECTS (1) cards (without the words on the back) and a set of OBJECTS (2) cards.
- They should shuffle them together and spread them out face down on the table.
- Player 1 should turn up two cards. If she can state a similarity between them, e.g. *'They both feel slippery'* or *'They both taste salty'*, she can keep them.
- If not, she leaves the cards face up, and the turn passes to Player 2.
- The next and subsequent players turn up two cards each time, but are allowed to find similarities between those two and any other cards which are lying face up.
- **The object of the game is to match up as many cards as possible.**
- The player with the most cards at the end is the winner.

20 Emotions

Topic area
adjectives for emotions

Vocabulary focus
happy, sad, worried, angry, delighted, surprised, frightened, nervous, impatient, proud, disappointed, hurt, jealous, curious, embarrassed, relieved, grateful, puzzled, fed up, shocked

Extra vocabulary
exam, holiday, detective, fail, pass, win, competition, shining, party, skiing, dropped, crash, climbing. (Also any vocabulary requested in Game 2.)

Structures
be, have got, simple present, *it makes me* + adjective, present perfect (for recognition only, not production)

Materials and preparation
GAME 1 Copy two sets of EMOTIONS PICTURES sheets per group of 4–5 students. Cut one sheet into individual emotions cards and the other into LOTTO BOARDS with four emotions on each. Cut the words off the LOTTO BOARDS.

GAME 2 None.

GAME 3 Copy one set of the EMOTIONS PICTURES sheets for each group of 3–4 students. Cut them into individual emotions cards; cut the words off the cards. Copy and cut up one set of SITUATIONS cards for each group.

How to use the games
GAME 1 Memorising
small group lotto game
- Divide students into groups of 4–5 and give each group a set of 20 EMOTIONS PICTURES cards (with words) and a set of LOTTO BOARDS (without words).
- Each student should take a lotto board.
- The emotions cards should be placed in a bag.
- Students should take it in turns to take a card from the bag without showing it to the others and to say the word on the card.
- The student who has the matching face on his lotto board can take the card and place it on his lotto board.
- **The object of the game is to find all the faces that match the words on the lotto board.**
- The player who fills his board first is the winner.
- The game can be played in a harder version by cutting the words off the emotions cards as well as the lotto boards.

GAME 2 Personalising
pairwork discussion
- Put up a questionnaire on the board:

WHAT MAKES YOU:

happy? sad? worried? angry? delighted? surprised? frightened? nervous? impatient? proud? disappointed? hurt? jealous? curious? embarrassed? relieved? grateful? puzzled? fed up? shocked?

- Give some of your own examples, e.g. *'Sunshine makes me happy'*, *'Big dogs make me nervous'*.
- Students should write short answers to the questionnaire (one or two words).
- Circulate to supply vocabulary.
- When they have finished, group them in pairs to share answers.

GAME 3 Communicating
small group matching game   RULES SHEET
Wow!
- Divide students into groups of 3–4.
- Give each group a set of EMOTIONS PICTURES cards and a set of SITUATIONS cards.

- They should put the situations cards face down in a pile in the middle of the table and deal out the emotions pictures equally.

- **The object of the game is to find a connection between the emotions cards and the situations cards.**

- Player 1 begins by turning up a situation card, e.g. *'You've done well in your exam'*. He tries to find an emotion card from his hand to connect with this and make a sentence, e.g. *'I'm feeling so happy/surprised/ delighted/proud/relieved – I passed my exam!'*

- If the group accept the sentence, he can throw away both cards. If not, he must retain the emotion card and replace the situation card at the bottom of the pile.

- Then the turn passes to the next player.

- The player who gets rid of his cards first is the winner.

21 Personality

Topic area
adjectives for personalities

Vocabulary focus
calm, emotional, funny, serious, gentle, rough, kind, unkind, generous, mean, polite, rude, good-tempered, bad-tempered, sociable, shy, confident, nervous, adventurous, domestic, miserable, jolly, decisive, indecisive

Extra vocabulary
astronaut, surgeon, clown, bank manager, teacher, nurse, president, robber, pilot, actor, fire fighter, journalist

Structures
be, have got, simple present (*we need …*), present continuous (*we're looking for …*)

Materials and preparation
GAME 1 Copy and cut up one set of PERSONALITIES cards per pair of students.

GAME 2 None.

GAME 3 Copy and cut up one set of JOBS cards and one set of CANDIDATES cards for each group of 3–4 students.

How to use the games
GAME 1 Memorising
pairwork sorting and matching games
- Divide students into pairs. Give each pair a set of PERSONALITIES cards.

- Ask them to spread out the cards face up on the table.

- They should first sort the cards into two groups: *positive* and *negative* personality characteristics.

- Students should work together to complete the task. Some words will fall clearly into one or the other category, others may provoke discussion!

- Then they should place all the cards face down on the table.

- They should take it in turns to turn up a card.

- **The object of the game is to find pairs of opposites.**

- When they turn up a card that is opposite in meaning to one already lying face up, the first person to name the two personality characteristics can keep the cards.

- The winner is the player with most cards at the end.

GAME 2 Personalising
pairwork discussion
- Tell students a little about the characteristics of people in your family.

- Then put them in pairs to talk about their own families' personalities.

GAME 3 Communicating
small group matching game   RULES SHEET
Rivals
- Put students in groups of 3–4.

- Give each group a set of JOBS cards and a set of CANDIDATES cards.

- They should put the jobs cards face down in the middle of the table and deal out the candidates cards equally.

- Each student should look at his hand of candidates cards and decide on three personality characteristics for each candidate. He should write them on the back of each card.

- **The object of the game is to match candidates with suitable jobs.**

- Player 1 begins by turning up a job card and announcing the job. She should also say what kind of person she thinks is suitable, e.g. *'We need an astronaut. We're looking for someone adventurous, confident and very calm.'*

- The other three players can press their claims, e.g. *'Tom here is very calm and decisive. You need someone decisive.'*

- It is up to Player 1 to choose the most suitable candidate for the job. The player with the successful candidate can discard that candidate card.

- Then it is the next player's turn to turn up a job card.

- The player who gets jobs for all her candidates first is the winner.

22 Travel

Topic area
travel

Vocabulary focus
hand luggage: *ticket, passport, visa, money, traveller's cheques, guidebook, foreign currency*

people: *passenger, driver, guard, ticket collector, customs official, pilot, stewardess, captain, bursar, crew*

terminals: *station, airport, ferry terminal, coach station*

places at terminals: *platform, waiting room, departure lounge, departure bay, departure gate / boarding gate*

checkpoints: *passport control, customs, ticket desk, check in*

Extra vocabulary
information desk, baggage check, depart, realise, change money, flight, delay, runway, embarkation, sail, announcement, cancelled, signal failures, complicated query, holding up

Structures
simple present (*you realise that …*), simple past (*we got on the train*), present perfect (*you've missed your coach*), imperatives (*go straight to …, throw a five, miss a go*), get (*get on the coach, get to the station, get your ticket*)

Materials and preparation

GAME 1 Copy and cut up one set of TRAVEL WORDS cards per pair of students. The cards below the solid line are extras – keep them separate.

GAME 2 None.

GAME 3 Copy and cut up one set of four TOKENS, one set of four JOURNEYS cards, and one MISSED CONNECTIONS board, per group of 6–8 students. You will need dice: one per group.

How to use the games

GAME 1 Memorising
pairwork sorting game
- Divide students into pairs.

- Give each pair a set of TRAVEL WORDS cards *without* the extras (below the solid line).

- Ask them to spread out the cards on the table, face up.

- **The object of the game is to sort the cards into five groups: *hand luggage, people, terminals, places at terminals, checkpoints*.**

- When they have done this, ask them to put aside the cards for *hand luggage* and *checkpoints* and to collect up the other three groups into a single pile.

- Give each pair the extra words cards and ask them to add them to the pile of cards for *people, terminals* and *places at terminals*.

- Ask them to sort this pile out again into four different groups: *train, coach, ferry, plane*. (Students in land-locked countries will make some different choices from those in countries where water forms a border.)

GAME 2 Personalising
pairwork visualisation
- Put the students into pairs.

- Ask all the students to close their eyes and think of a journey by public transport that they remember, perhaps because it was particularly difficult, exciting, interesting, unusual, uncomfortable or complicated.

- Ask them to remember the stages of their journey in detail.

- Then ask them to open their eyes and tell their partner about their journey.

GAME 3 Communicating
small group board game
Missed connections

Long game

RULES SHEET

- Put students in groups of 6–8.

- Give each group a MISSED CONNECTIONS board, one set of four TOKENS, a set of 24 JOURNEYS cards (in separate packs: coach, train, ferry and plane), and a dice.

- Students get into pairs. Each pair chooses a token (coach, train, ferry or plane) and places it on the appropriate terminal (the first four squares at the bottom of the board, after 'Home').

- They take their appropriate pack of journey cards (coach, train, ferry or plane) and place it face down in front of them so that the card numbered 1 is on the top and the rest follow in order 1–6.

- Players play in pairs.

- The first pair starts by turning over their top card (number 1) and following the instructions.

- Each time they need to throw the dice, they can try twice (once per player) to get the number they need.

- One of the pair must throw the exact number required, so that they move only onto their own squares. (E.g. the train pair cannot 'rest' on a coach square.)

- If they do not throw the required number, the turn passes to the next pair.

- **The object of the game is to get to the end of the journey as quickly as possible.**

- The cards will guide them round the board, from 'Home' to 'Depart', telling the story of the start of their journey.

- The pair who get to 'Depart' first are the winners.

- When the game is over, each pair should tell the others the story of how their journey started, using the cards to help them remember.

23 Television

Topic area
watching TV, types of programme, opinions of programmes

Vocabulary focus
watching TV: *programme, aerial, channel, satellite, cable, remote control, turn on/off, turn up/down, go over to another channel, adjust, volume, tune*

programme types: *sitcom (situation comedy), drama, documentary, fly-on-the-wall documentary/docu-soap, comedy show, cookery programme, health programme, chat show, news programme, soap (opera), sports programme, current affairs programme, game show, quiz show, cartoon, film/movie, interview, arts programme, music programme, serial, wildlife programme, travel programme, children's programme, magazine programme*

opinions: *interesting, stimulating, boring, rubbish, funny, gripping, exciting, trivial*

Extra vocabulary
(Provided in the PROGRAMMES sheet – Game 3):
animated, tonight's edition, starring, profile, presented by, hosted by, feature, featuring. Students do not need to produce this or other unfamiliar vocabulary.

Structures
would like/rather/prefer, want to …, can/could you …?

Materials and preparation

GAME 1 Decide which set(s) of vocabulary you want to practise: *watching TV* or *programme types.*

For *watching TV*: Copy and cut up one set of TELEVISION WORDS cards and one set of TELEVISION PICTURES cards for each pair of students.

For *programme types*: Copy and cut up one set of PROGRAMME TYPES cards and one set of PROGRAMMES cards for each group of 3–4.

GAME 2 Copy one set of PROGRAMME TYPES cards per student and one set of OPINIONS cards per pair.

GAME 3 You need material for large groups (not fewer than 6 and not more than 11). Copy and cut up one set of FAMILY ROLES cards for each group and one complete PROGRAMMES page per pair.

How to use the games

GAME 1 Memorising
1 pairwork matching game: *Watching TV*
- Divide your class into pairs.
- Give each pair a set of TELEVISION WORDS cards.
- Ask them to put the cards in a pile face down on the table.
- Give them a set of TELEVISION PICTURES cards.
- Ask them to spread out the pictures face up on the table.

- **The object of the game is to match words and pictures.**
- The first player should turn up a card from the pile and make a request based on that phrase, e.g. *'Can you adjust the aerial, please?'*
- The first to produce the matching picture, saying, *'Yes, all right!'* can keep the pair of cards.
- Then it is the next player's turn.
- The player with most cards at the end is the winner.

2 small group matching game: *Programme types*
- Divide your class into groups of 3–4.
- Give each group a set of PROGRAMME TYPES cards and a set of PROGRAMMES cards.
- They should deal out four cards from each set to all players.
- The remainder of the cards should be shuffled together and placed in a pile face down in the middle of the table.
- **The object of the game is to match programme types and programmes.**
- Player 1 begins by selecting a programme type from his hand (e.g. *documentary*).
- He then asks any other player, *'Is there a (good) documentary on tonight?'*
- If the player has a corresponding programme card she should give it to him, saying, e.g., *'Yes, there's "Our Working Lives" at six o'clock.'*
- The two matching cards can then be laid down as a 'trick'.
- If not, he must take a card from the pile.
- Then it is the next player's turn.
- The player with most 'tricks' at the end is the winner.

GAME 2 Personalising
pairwork discussion
- Give each student a set of PROGRAMME TYPES cards.
- Ask them to arrange these in order of preference.
- When they have finished, ask them to show their arrangement to the person next to them and to discuss their preferences.
- Give each pair a set of OPINIONS cards.
- Ask them to group the programme types under the different opinions and to discuss any differences of opinion.

GAME 3 Communicating
large group arranging game
Telly addicts

Long game

- Divide your class into groups of 6–11 students.
- Give each group enough complete pages of PROGRAMMES for there to be one between two players.
- Give each group a set of FAMILY ROLES cards.

- Tell them they live in a house where there are two TV sets, one upstairs and one downstairs.

- **The object of the game is to sort themselves into two groups – one for each TV – and to decide what they will watch.**

- To do this they will have to discuss their likes and dislikes and come to an arrangement where everyone is happy.

24 Holidays

Topic area
holiday types and activities

Vocabulary focus
types of holiday: *skiing, camping, caravanning, safari, seaside, beach, hiking, cycling, coach tour, cruise, self-catering, apartment, villa, hotel*

activities: *sunbathing, sightseeing, buying souvenirs, exploring, sailing, surfing, windsurfing, snorkelling, trying the local food, going to bars and discos, getting fresh air and exercise, meeting people and learning about other cultures*

clichés: *exotic, lively, thrilling, peaceful, crowded, relaxing, touristy, off the beaten track, picturesque, adventure, noisy, (get) away from it all, glorious, romantic, stunning, idyllic, friendly*

Extra vocabulary
water sports, nightlife, trek, trekking, price limit, ready-erected, locations, half board, accommodation, sophisticated, bungalow, scenery, barge, pre-book, studio, guided tour, stress, health farm, white-water rafting, yacht, basics, luxury

Structures
simple past, *I'd like … , I'm looking for … , What about … ?, How about … ?*

Materials and preparation

GAME 1 Decide which set(s) of vocabulary you want to practise: *types of holiday, activities* or *clichés*.

For *types of holiday*: Copy and cut up one set of HOLIDAY TYPES and one set of POSTCARDS for each pair of students.

For *activities*: Copy and cut up one set of ACTIVITIES cards for each group of 3–4.

For *clichés*: Copy and cut up one set of POSTCARDS and one set of CLICHÉS cards for each group of 3–4.

GAME 2 None.

GAME 3 Copy three sheets of TRAVEL AGENTS and cut them into three sections: A, B and C.

If you have more than 36 students in your class, alter the wording on the TRAVEL AGENTS sheets so that each holiday has 'only *2 places* remaining'.

Now for some maths!

Mentally divide the number of students in your class by three: one third will be travel agents and two thirds will be holidaymakers. Copy and cut up enough HOLIDAYMAKERS cards for two thirds of the class to have one card each. Put them in a bag.

How to use the games
GAME 1 Memorising
1 pairwork matching game: *Types of holiday*
- Divide your class into pairs.

- Give each pair a set of HOLIDAY TYPES and a set of POSTCARDS.

- Get them to put the postcards in a pile face down on the table and to spread out the phrases face up.

- They should take it in turns to turn up a postcard from the pile.

- **The object of the game is to match the phrases and pictures.**

- The first person to say the phrase that describes the picture can keep both cards.

- The player with most cards at the end is the winner.

2 small group guessing game: *Activities*
- Divide students into groups of 3–4.

- Give each group a set of ACTIVITIES cards.

- Get them to put these face down in a pile in the middle of the table.

- The first player should take a card and, without showing it to the others, should mime the activity.

- **The object of the game is to guess the activity being mimed.**

- The first student to guess correctly can keep the card.

- The student with most cards at the end is the winner.

3 small group matching game: *Clichés*
- Divide your class into groups of 3–4.

- Give each group a set of POSTCARDS and a set of CLICHÉS.

- They should put the postcards face down in a pile in the middle of the table and deal out the clichés equally to all players.

- They should turn up the first postcard.

- **The object of the game is to match postcards and clichés.**

- The player who produces a suitable cliché first can keep both cards.

- There may be more than one appropriate cliché for each postcard.

- If the other players think they have a more suitable cliché, they can argue the case!

- The player with most cards at the end is the winner.

GAME 2 Personalising
pairwork visualisation

- Ask students to close their eyes and imagine they are on holiday. It can be any kind of holiday they like – list a few types.

- Tell them to imagine it is the end of the afternoon. What did they do during the day? (List a few activities.) What are they going to do this evening?

- If they could choose one word (or phrase) to describe their holiday, what would it be? (Suggest some of the words in the clichés cards.)

- Then get them to open their eyes and describe their holiday to a partner.

GAME 3 Communicating   `Long game`
whole class matching game
Hard sell

- Divide your class into approximately one third and two thirds.

- Divide the one third into three groups. Tell them they are three travel agents.

- Put each group at a table in a different area of the classroom.

- Give each travel agent a different list of holidays: TRAVEL AGENTS sheet A, B or C.

- Ask them to invent a name for themselves and to make a paper sign.

- Tell the remaining two thirds that they are holidaymakers who want to book a holiday each.

- Go round with a bag of HOLIDAYMAKERS cards and get them to take one each.

- **The object of the game is for the holidaymakers to get the holiday they like best and for the travel agents to sell as many holidays as possible.**

- To do this the holidaymakers will have to go round the classroom asking the travel agents what they have available. (*'I'm looking for ...'*, *'I'd like ...'*)

- The travel agents should make an effort to sell their holidays - they can invent extra details if they like. (*'What about ...'*, *'How about ...'*)

- When the holidaymakers decide on a holiday, they should go back and 'book' it if it is not sold out.

- If the holiday they want is sold out, they will have to try another agent.

- The travel agents should keep count of how many holidays they have sold, by marking their holidays sheet. (If there are more than 36 in the class, they should have two places available on each holiday.)

- The travel agency that sells most holidays is the winner.

25 Work

Topic area
work activities, hours, pay and conditions

Vocabulary focus
activities: *type, do word processing, write reports, sell, sign, attend meetings, do the accounts, interview, be in charge of, supervise, train, answer phone calls, meet clients, repair, install, fit, invoice, work on an assembly line, operate machinery, check, invent, create, research into, draw up plans, design, examine, diagnose, treat, operate on, look after, care for, collect, deliver*

conditions: *salary, pay, income, regular hours, shift work, flexitime, full time, part time, jobshare, on nights, night shift, overtime, apply for, employer, employee, self-employed, trainee, apprentice, pay rise, salary increase, promotion, prospects, job security, temporary, permanent, pension scheme, resign, get the sack, be fired, unemployed, out of work, retire*

Extra vocabulary
artistic, health, administrative, factory, manual, scientific; names of jobs are provided in Game 3 (e.g. *accountant, architect*)

Structures
simple present, simple past

Materials and preparation

GAME 1 Decide which set(s) of vocabulary you want to practise: *activities* or *conditions*.

For *activities*: Copy and cut up one set of ACTIVITIES cards for each pair of students. Don't forget to copy the words on the back.

For *conditions*: Copy and cut up one set of CONDITIONS cards for each group of 3–4. Don't forget to copy the definitions on the back.

GAME 2 Copy one QUESTIONNAIRE for each student in the class.

GAME 3 Make two copies of the LOTTO page for each group of 3–4. Cut one set up into four boards with four pictures on each board. Cut the other set up into 16 pictures and put them in a bag.

NOTE: The LOTTO cards have names of the jobs below the pictures. If you want to play the game in a more challenging version, make one copy of the cards and white out the names of the jobs. Then use this as your master copy and follow the instructions above.

How to use the games
GAME 1 Memorising
1 pairwork matching and sorting: *Activities*
- Divide your class into pairs.

- Give each pair a set of ACTIVITIES cards.

- Get them to lay the cards out picture-side up.

- They should take it in turns to choose one and think of a verb phrase that describes it, e.g. *meet clients*.

- **The object of the game is to match phrases and pictures.**

- When they have said the phrase they think corresponds to the picture, they may turn the card over.

- If they have identified it correctly, they should leave the card word-side up; if they are wrong, they should turn the card back over again.

- When all the cards are word-side up, put the following headings on the board:

WORKING WITH - PEOPLE
               INFORMATION / IDEAS
               THINGS

- Ask students to sort the cards into these groups.

- You could ask them to sort them into these headings instead, or in addition:

ARTISTIC   HEALTH   ADMINISTRATIVE
FACTORY   MANUAL   SCIENTIFIC

2 small group quiz: *Conditions*

- Divide students into groups of 3–4.

- Give each group a set of CONDITIONS cards.

- Get them to put these in a pile, number-side up.

- They should take it in turns to take one card from the pile and read out the phrase to the rest of the group.

- **The object of the game is to give the right definition.**

- The student who gives the correct definition can keep the card. They can check that the definition is correct by turning the card over.

- If no one can give the definition or the wrong definition is given, the student posing the question can read out the definition to the others and then replace the card at the bottom of the pile.

- Then it is the next player's turn.

- The player with the most cards at the end is the winner.

- When they have finished, they can play the game in a harder version by placing the cards in a pile definition-side up.

GAME 2 Personalising
pairwork discussion

- Give each student a QUESTIONNAIRE.

- Get them to fill it in for themselves.

- Then put them in pairs to compare their answers with a partner.

VARIATION: If you like, you can give students a second questionnaire after they have filled in their own, and ask them to imagine what replies their partner would write. Then, when they discuss their answers, they can compare what they actually wrote with their partner's image of them.

GAME 3 Communicating
small group lotto game
Job lottery

- Divide your class into groups of 3–4.

- Give each group a set of four LOTTO boards and a bag of the individual cards.

- Each player should take one board.

- The first player dips her hand into the bag and takes a card.

- Without showing the other players or telling them the name of the job, she must describe a few things about it to the others, e.g. *'She doesn't get a very good salary. She often has to work long hours and do night duty. Her job involves caring for other people.'*

- **The object of the game is to guess the job and match it with one of the pictures on the lotto board.**

- The player with a picture that matches the description can ask to see the card, saying, e.g. *'Is she a nurse?'* If the picture matches, he can place it on his board.

- Then it is the next player's turn to dip into the bag and get a job card.

- The player who covers all his pictures first is the winner.

- If a player dips into the bag and gets one of her own pictures she must put it back and take another.

26 Crime

Topic area
criminals and criminal offences

Vocabulary focus
criminals and crimes: *arsonist, arson, drug dealer, drug dealing, vandal, vandalism, burglar, burglary, housebreaker, housebreaking, hijacker, hijacking, mugger, mugging, blackmailer, blackmail, fraudster, fraud, terrorist, bomb attack, thief, theft/stealing, robber, (armed) robbery, murderer, murder, rapist, rape, shoplifter, shoplifting, kidnapper, kidnapping, forger, forgery, smuggler, smuggling, (football) hooligan, hooliganism, assailant, assault*

detection: *commit, investigate, trace, arrest, question, detain, release, charge someone with*

Extra vocabulary
cell, inmate, fireworks, clanging, box of matches, suspicious, drugs, break into, steal, smash up, threaten, hit, deceive, false, ransom, pick a fight, champion boxer, destroy, blow up, kill, force, sex

Structures
simple present, simple past

Materials and preparation

GAME 1 Decide which set(s) of vocabulary you want your class to practise: *criminals and crimes* or *detection*.

For *criminals and crimes*: Copy and cut up one set of CRIMINALS and CRIMES cards per pair of students. Make sure you copy the two sheets back-to-back.

For *detection*: Copy and cut up one set of DETECTION cards per pair.

GAME 2 Copy and cut up enough MUGSHOTS for each student to have one picture.

GAME 3 Copy one PRISON PLAN for each student. Copy and cut up enough INMATES for each student to have one role card.

NOTE: There are 14 cards and 14 cells on the plan. If you have fewer than 14 students, reduce the number of cards and white out cells from the plan, from number 14 downwards in sequence. (Make sure the cards you discard correspond to the cells you are not using – see ANSWERS at the end of the teacher's notes.) On the highest-numbered of your remaining cards, cross off the second paragraph.

If you have more than 14 students, play in two groups, or tell the class some cells have two inmates. (They will both have committed the same crime.)

How to use the games

GAME 1 Memorising

1 pairwork matching game: *Criminals and crimes*
- Divide your class into pairs.
- Give each pair a set of CRIMINALS/CRIMES cards.
- They should lay them out number-side up (criminals).
- Ask them to try to remember the names of the related crimes.
- **The object of the game is to match the criminal to the crime.**
- Player 1 should take a card and give the name of the related crime (e.g. *arsonist – arson*). She can check by looking at the back.
- If she was right, she can keep the card.
- The player with most cards at the end is the winner.

2 small group guessing game: *Criminals and crimes*
- Then join the pairs together with other pairs to make groups of 3–4.
- Ask them to put one set of their cards in a paper bag (or put them in a pile, number-side up, and cover the pile with a piece of paper).
- Player 1 takes a card, looks at the numbered (criminal) side, and, without showing it to the others, tells the others something about the criminal, e.g. *'This person needs a box of matches for her crime,'* or *'This person gets drunk and fights people at football matches.'*

- **The object of the game is to guess the related crime (e.g. *arson*, *hooliganism*).**
- The player who guesses correctly can keep the card.
- The player with most cards at the end is the winner.

3 pairwork guessing game: *Detection*
- Divide students into pairs.
- Give each pair a set of DETECTION cards
- They should first divide the cards into two groups – those words which would complete the phrase '… *a crime'* and those words which would complete the phrase '… *a criminal'*.
- They should then arrange the cards in the order these events would usually take place.

GAME 2 Personalising
pairwork writing and discussion
- Give each student a MUGSHOTS picture.
- Ask them to imagine this picture is on the front page of a newspaper.
- Get them to imagine what crime the criminal committed and to write a headline and brief news report.
- Then put them in pairs to discuss their ideas.
- If you like, you can pin the pictures and 'news reports' around the room and get students to go round and read them.

GAME 3 Communicating
whole class search game
What's my crime?

`Long game`

- Give everyone in the class a PRISON PLAN and an INMATES role card.
- **The object of the game is to find out what criminals are in which cells – and thus what your own crime is!**
- To do this they will have to get up and move around the class exchanging information about the inmates on either side of them.
- When they have completed the prison plan by writing a type of criminal in each cell (e.g. *mugger*), they can sit down.

ANSWERS: 1 arsonist **2** mugger **3** smuggler **4** housebreaker/burglar **5** vandal **6** hijacker **7** blackmailer **8** thief **9** armed robber/bank robber **10** fraudster **11** shoplifter **12** kidnapper **13** forger **14** (football) hooligan

27 The law

Topic area
the legal system

Vocabulary focus
police/legal procedures: *investigate (a crime), arrest (a suspect), charge with (a crime), make a statement, be remanded in custody, be released on bail, brief (a barrister), appear in court, be accused of, plead (innocent/guilty), be tried (for a crime/an offence), give/hear evidence, put the case for (the prosecution/the defence), sum up, reach a verdict, pass a sentence, prosecute, defend*

people: *police officer, counsel for the prosecution/the defence, barrister, solicitor, judge, defendant/accused, witnesses, jury*

Extra vocabulary
lawyer, car salesman, original (= first), stick up for, swear, mate (= friend), clear-cut, evidence, contradictory, cash, screeched to a halt, suspicions, sinister, hang about, stand by/stick by someone, convincing, cross-examine

Structures
simple past, present continuous, time clauses with *as*, *when* and *while*, *could/couldn't have*

Materials and preparation

GAME 1 Decide which set(s) of vocabulary you want to practise: *police/legal procedures* alone, or *procedures* and *people*.

For *police/legal procedures*: Copy and cut up one set of PROCEDURES cards per pair of students in your class.

For *procedures* and *people*: Copy and cut up one set of PROCEDURES cards and one set of PEOPLE cards per group of 3–4.

GAME 2 Copy one COURTROOM SCENE per pair of students.

GAME 3 Play with a minimum of 12 students. Copy and cut up one set of role cards for THE TRIAL OF RONNIE SMALLS. If you have more than 12 students, copy extra Jury cards. If you have more than 30 or so, play in two groups.

How to use the games
GAME 1 Memorising
1 pairwork ordering game: *Procedures*
- Divide your class into pairs.

- Give each group a set of PROCEDURES cards.

- Get them to shuffle the cards and then to spread them out face up on the desk.

- **The object of the game is to put the cards in the order in which they would take place.**

- The pair who get the correct order first are the winners.

ANSWER: The correct order reads from left to right across the rows on the master sheet.

2 small group matching game: *People and procedures*
- Divide your class into groups of 3–4.

- Give each group a set of PROCEDURES cards and a set of PEOPLE cards.

- Ask them to put the procedures cards face down in a pile in the middle of the table and to spread out the people cards face up on the table.

- **The object of the game is to match procedures and people.**

- Players should take it in turns to take a card from the pile and ask a question about who does the action, e.g. *'Who passes the sentence?'*

- The first player who finds the appropriate card on the table and gives the correct answer at the same time, e.g. *'The judge'*, can keep both cards.

- The player with most cards at the end is the winner.

ANSWERS: The correct answers can be seen on the two master sheets, where the procedure and related person appear in the same position.

GAME 2 Personalising
pairwork visualisation and discussion
- Give each pair of students a COURTROOM SCENE picture.

- Ask them to imagine, silently:

  What crime is the defendant being tried for?
  What question did the lawyer/barrister put?
  What is the witness saying?
  What are the jury thinking?
  What verdict will they come to?
  What sentence will the judge pass?

- You can put the questions on the board, if you prefer, or ask the questions orally, pausing after each question to give the students time to think.

- Ask them to share their ideas with a partner when they have finished.

GAME 3 Communicating   `Long game`
whole class role play game
Trial by jury
- Play this game with the whole class (minimum 12).

- Give each person a role card for THE TRIAL OF RONNIE SMALLS on pages 126 and 127.

- Give them a little time to read their cards.

- While they are busy reading, send the defence witnesses out of the classroom. Everyone else should stay.

- Go with the defence witnesses and tell them they can discuss their roles and make up their stories together.

- Go back to the classroom and get everyone in position and start the trial.

- Let the judge run the trial. The witnesses should come in one at a time when they are called.

- **The object of the game is for the jury to decide if the accused is innocent or guilty.**

28 Education

Topic area
school and university

Vocabulary focus
places: *nursery, playgroup, primary/secondary/grammar/ comprehensive/high school, college, university, private, independent, public, state*

people and courses: (school:) *pupil, teacher, subject, lesson, A levels, GCSEs*; (university:) *student, lecturer, course, lecture, tutorial, seminar, graduate, degree*

types: *strict, liberal, progressive, traditional, formal, informal, disciplined, free, rebel, conformist, bully, victim, shy, outgoing, insecure, confident, unpopular, popular*

Extra vocabulary
vocabulary for emotions, *selected, establishment, fee-paying, non-fee-paying, academic, qualifications, practical, exam, organised*

Structures
simple past

Materials and preparation

GAME 1 Decide which set(s) of vocabulary you want your class to practise: *places*, or *people and courses*, or *types*.

For *places*: Copy and cut up two sets of PLACES cards and two DEFINITIONS sheets for each group of 3–4.

For *people and courses*: Copy and cut up one set of PEOPLE AND COURSES cards per pair of students.

For *types*: Copy and cut up one set of OPPOSITES cards per pair of students.

GAME 2 None.

GAME 3 Copy one COINCIDENCES sheet for every student in the class. (The sheet is printed twice on the page.)

How to use the games

GAME 1 Memorising
1 small group matching game: *Places*
- Divide your class into groups of 3–4.

- Give each group two sets of PLACES cards and one or two copies of the DEFINITIONS sheet.

- They should keep the definitions to one side for reference and place one set of places cards in a pile face down and spread the other set face up on the table.

- The students should take it in turns to take a card from the pile.

- Without saying the word on the card, they should give a definition: e.g. (picking up *primary school*) '*A school for children under 11 years old.*'

- **The object of the game is to match places and definitions.**

- The first player who picks up the appropriate card from the table and says the name can keep both cards.

- In case of a difference of opinion, they should refer to the definitions sheet.

- The player with most cards at the end is the winner.

2 pairwork sorting game: *People and courses*
- Divide students into pairs.

- Give each pair a set of PEOPLE AND COURSES cards.

- **The object of the game is for all pairs to sort them as quickly as possible into two sets: *school* and *university*.**

- The team who do this first are the winners.

3 pairwork matching game: *Types*
- Divide students into pairs.

- Give each pair a set of OPPOSITES cards.

- Ask them to place these face down on the table and to take turns in turning them up, one at a time.

- **The object of the game is to match opposites.**

- When a player turns up a card that is the opposite to one that is already face up, the first person to say both words can take the cards.

- The person with most cards at the end is the winner.

GAME 2 Personalising
pairwork visualisation
- Ask students to close their eyes and think back to their schooldays – primary or secondary.

- Ask them to visualise:

  a teacher they had, and to remember what they felt about him or her
  a friend they had
  someone they didn't like
  an incident they remember clearly

- Then ask them to open their eyes and tell a partner about it.

GAME 3 Communicating `Long game`
whole class matching game
Well I never!
- Give a COINCIDENCES sheet to everyone in the class.

- Ask them to invent and write a short *imaginary* account of their education, including (in any order and any combination) the words they have been given.

- When they have finished, ask them to stand up and move around talking to each other as if at a party.

- Tell them they are at a party where they don't know anyone, but they might find people they have something in common with.

- **The object of the game is to find another person sharing as many coincidences as possible.**

- They should keep a note of the number of similarities (e.g. same school, same subject at university, same likes and dislikes, same best friend, etc.) that they find with each person they talk to.

- Set a time limit, say, 15 minutes.

- Stop the game at the end of this time. The pair who have found most coincidences wins.

29 Relationships

Topic area
human relationships

Vocabulary focus
events: *fall in love, (get) divorced, go out with, (get) engaged, get married, live together, separate(d), break/split up, be attracted to, start a family, (get) pregnant, find a new partner, have an affair*

people: *husband, wife, partner, girlfriend, boyfriend, fiancé(e), ex-husband, ex-wife, stepmother, stepfather, a gay couple, lover, mistress, single parent*

being together: *faithful, trust, sense of humour, a lot in common, calm, patient, tolerant, work at, argue, grow apart, lead separate lives, get on each other's nerves, drive mad, drive up the wall, annoy, irritating habits*

Extra vocabulary
extra-marital, live with, happily married, household, avid, coincidentally, domestic bliss, jealous, house-share, episode, something between them, admit, mystified, muddled, to miss someone

Structures
present continuous, present perfect, simple past, *going to, will, would*

Materials and preparation

GAME 1 Decide which set(s) of vocabulary you want your students to practise: *events, people* or *being together*.

For *events*: Copy and cut up one set of EVENTS cards for each pair of students.

For *people*: Copy and cut up one set of PEOPLE cards for each group of 3–4. Don't forget to copy the DEFINITIONS on the back.

For *being together*: Copy and cut up one set of BEING TOGETHER cards for each pair of students.

GAME 2 Copy a QUESTIONNAIRE for each student in the class. (These are printed on the same sheet as the map for Game 3.)

GAME 3 Play with 6 or more students. Copy and cut up enough WATCHING *COMMOTION STREET* cards for each

student to have one. Make sure that at least one example of each card 1–6 is handed out. Copy enough sheets of the MAP OF *COMMOTION STREET* for every student to have one. (The questionnaire is for Game 2.)

How to use the games

GAME 1 Memorising

1 pairwork arranging game: *Events*
- Divide your class into pairs.

- Give each pair a set of EVENTS cards.

- Ask them to spread out the cards face up on the table.

- Ask them to imagine these are all stages in the life of one couple.

- **The object of the game is to arrange the cards in the order in which they think the events happened.**

- When they have done this, ask each pair to join up with another pair and compare orders, and discuss any differences.

- If there are no differences, or if you want to extend the activity, ask the students (before or after the pairs combine into groups) to make up the story of an imaginary couple based on the events in the order they have arranged them.

- These cards are deliberately not positioned in any suggested order on the master sheet.

2 small group matching game: *People*
- Divide your class into groups of 3–4.

- Give each group one set of PEOPLE cards.

- Ask them to put these in a pile, number-side up.

- Cover the pile with a piece of paper so that the top card is not visible, or put the cards in a paper bag.

- They should take it in turns to take the top card (or a card from the bag) and read out the word on the numbered side.

- **The object of the game is to give the right definition for the word.**

- The player who does so first can keep the card.

- Other players can challenge a definition and give a better definition. Definitions are on the back of the cards so they can check.

- The player with most cards at the end is the winner.

- The game can be played in a harder version by reading the cards definition-side.

3 pairwork sorting game: *Being together*
- Divide your class into pairs.

- Give each pair a set of BEING TOGETHER cards.

- Ask them to place the cards in a pile face down on the table.

- Write up on the board:

  We broke up because …   We stayed together because …

- **The object of the game is to divide the cards into these two categories**.

- Students should take it in turns to pick up a card from the pile and assign it to one of these two categories.

- Check answers with the whole class at the end.

GAME 2 Personalising
pairwork questionnaire and discussion
- Give each student a copy of the QUESTIONNAIRE.

- Ask them to fill it in for themselves.

- Then put them in pairs and ask them to share their answers and discuss question 4.

GAME 3 Communicating   `Long game`
whole class information gap game
Commotion Street
- Give everyone in the class a card from the WATCHING COMMOTION STREET sheet, making sure you give out at least one example of each of the cards 1–6.

- Tell them they have all watched a recent episode of the popular soap opera, *Commotion Street*.

- However, they have missed some episodes and are dying to know what happened in the gaps.

- Give them all a MAP OF COMMOTION STREET and ask them to read the instructions and fill it in from what they know from the background information. (Students with card 6 won't be able to fill much in!)

- Then ask them to get up and circulate, asking others if they saw any of the episodes they missed and getting them to share information.

- They record this on the map in diagrammatic form by drawing lines between the characters and writing in the relationship, as in the example *Belinda - Leo: divorced*.

- **The object of the game is to find out as much of the story as possible in 10 minutes**.

- When the time is up, put the students in random groups of 5–6 and ask them to share their information in order to reconstruct what happened in episodes 6–11.

- When they have done this, bring their information together in a class discussion.

- Then ask each group to discuss what will happen next – you can make this a writing exercise if you like.

30 Space

Topic area
heavenly bodies and space exploration

Vocabulary focus
heavenly bodies: *sun, moon, star, planet, galaxy, constellation, atmosphere, outer space, asteroid, comet*

exploration: *rocket, spaceship, space capsule, lunar module, probe, astronaut, space shuttle, mission control, launch pad, space station, satellite, UFO (= unidentified flying object), flying saucer, alien, extra-terrestrial, Martian*

Extra vocabulary
intelligent life, space exploration, benefits, universe, radar, asteroid shower, spacecraft, floating, control panel, screen, monsters, touchdown, colliding, collision, engine failure, stowaway

Structures
I think that …, conditions *(if … would, could, might, may),* present perfect, present continuous, *shall, should, ought to*

Materials and preparation
GAME 1 Decide which set(s) of vocabulary you want to practise: *heavenly bodies* or *exploration*.

For *heavenly bodies*: Copy and cut up one set of HEAVENLY BODIES labels and one STAR MAP per pair of students.

For *exploration*: Copy and cut up one set of SPACE labels and one SPACE EXPLORATION picture per group of 3–4 students.

GAME 2 Copy one QUESTIONNAIRE per student.

GAME 3 For each group of 3–4, copy one MISSION IMPOSSIBLE game board, and copy and cut up one complete set of STORY OF A MISSION cards (sheets 1 and 2). Give each group one counter and a dice.

How to use the games
GAME 1 Memorising
1 pairwork labelling game: *Heavenly bodies*
- Divide your class into pairs.

- Give each pair a set of HEAVENLY BODIES labels and a STAR MAP.

- Ask them to spread the labels face down on the table.

- **The object of the game is to label the star map correctly.**

- The first player should turn up a label from the table.

- If he knows where it goes on the picture, he can put it in the correct place. If not, he must replace it on the table.

- Then it is the other player's turn.

- The pair who finish first with all their labels in the correct place are the winners. Read them the answers so they can check at the end.

ANSWERS: 1 sun **2** moon **3** star **4** planet **5** galaxy **6** constellation **7** atmosphere **8** outer space **9** asteroid **10** comet

2 small group sorting and labelling games: *Exploration*

• Divide your class into groups of 3–4.

• Give each group a set of numbered SPACE labels.

• Ask them to spread these out face up on the table and to sort them into two groups: *science fact* and *science fiction*. (Write these headings up on the board and explain them if necessary.)

• They should then discard the science fiction labels (numbers 12-16: *UFO, flying saucer, alien, extra-terrestrial, Martian*).

• They turn the remaining labels over so they are all face down, and spread them on the table.

• Give each group a SPACE EXPLORATION picture.

• They should take it in turns to pick up a label from the table and, without showing it to the others, read out the word.

• The first person to say the number on the picture that corresponds to the number on the label can keep the label.

• The player with most labels at the end is the winner.

GAME 2 Personalising
pairwork questionnaire and discussion

• Give each student a QUESTIONNAIRE.

• Ask them to write down their answers to the questions.

• Then put them in pairs to discuss their answers.

GAME 3 Communicating
small group board game
Mission Impossible

Long game
RULES SHEET

• Divide your class into groups of 3–4.

• Give each group a MISSION IMPOSSIBLE board, a set of STORY OF A MISSION picture cards (30 cards) and a counter and dice.

• Ask the students to put the board in the middle of the table and put the counter on the square labelled *Blast off*.

• They should sort the cards into four piles – sun, planet, star and moon – and place them face down on the appropriate places around the board.

• Player 1 begins by throwing the dice and moving the counter the appropriate number of squares.

• He then picks up a card from the pile marked with the same symbol as the square he has landed on, and tells the others about the event pictured on it.

• The group should decide how to react and what to do.

• Then the next player throws the dice and moves the counter, and so on. The used cards should be laid out in a line to form a picture story as they go.

• **The object of the game is to get to the end of the board, building up a story on the way.**

• When all the groups have finished they can tell each other their stories, using the picture cards they have laid out as cues to help them remember.

The photocopiable games material and rules sheets follow on pages 39 to 144

1 Transport

VEHICLES

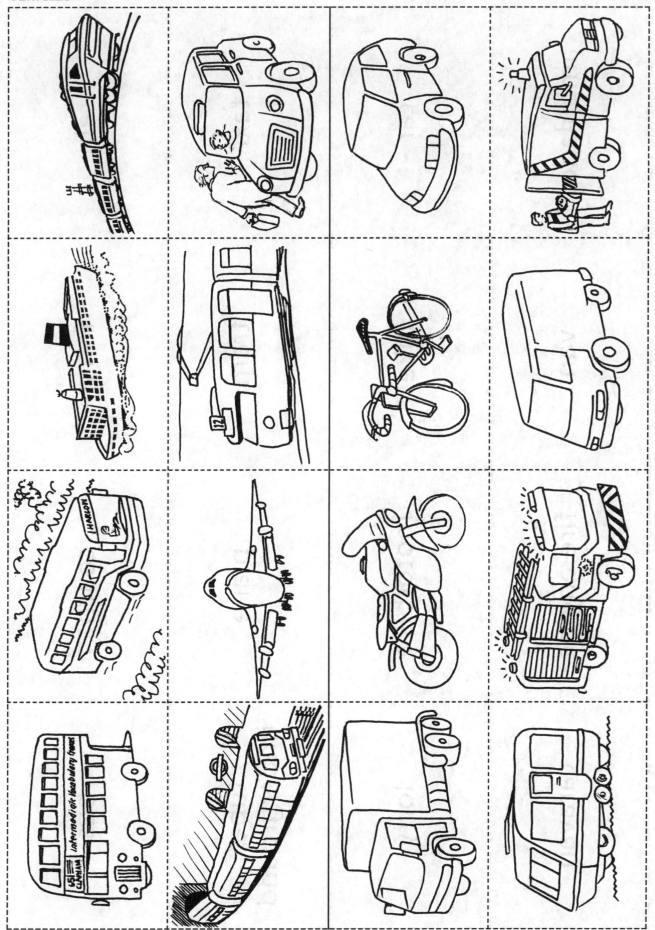

1 Transport

VEHICLES

ambulance	car	taxi	train
van	bike	tram	ferry
fire engine	motorbike	plane	coach
caravan	lorry	tube/underground	bus

1 Transport

PLACES

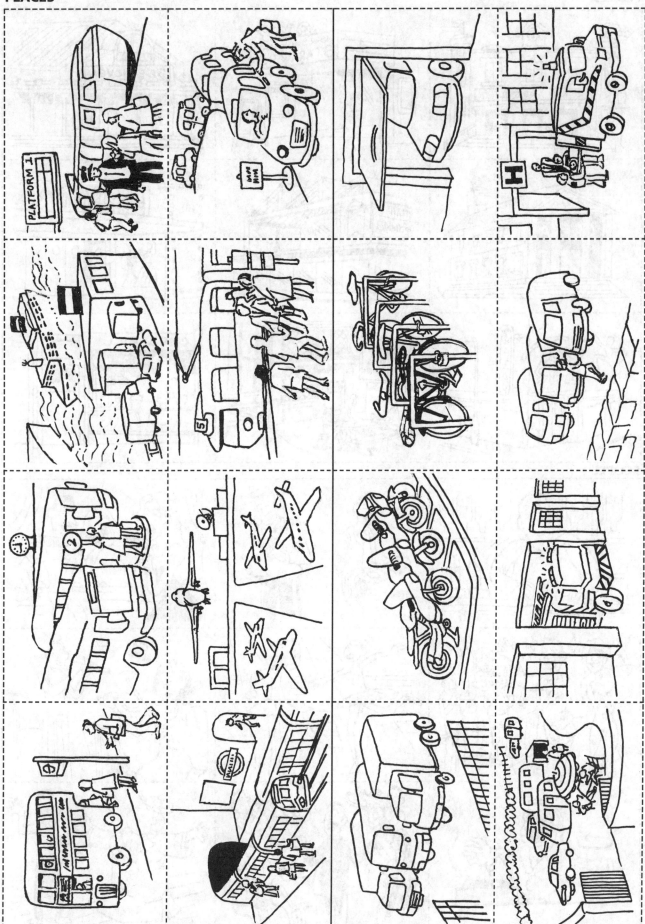

2 Entertainment

PLACES

PEOPLE

2 Entertainment

PLACES

concert hall	cinema	theatre
dance hall / ballroom	opera house	opera house
restaurant	pub	disco

PEOPLE

actors	waiters	barman
musicians	dancers	film stars
singers	band	disc jockey

2 Entertainment

EVENTS

2 Entertainment

EVENTS

meal	film	play
concert	ballet	drink
opera	dance	disco

EVENTS

2 Entertainment

TICKETS AND VOUCHERS

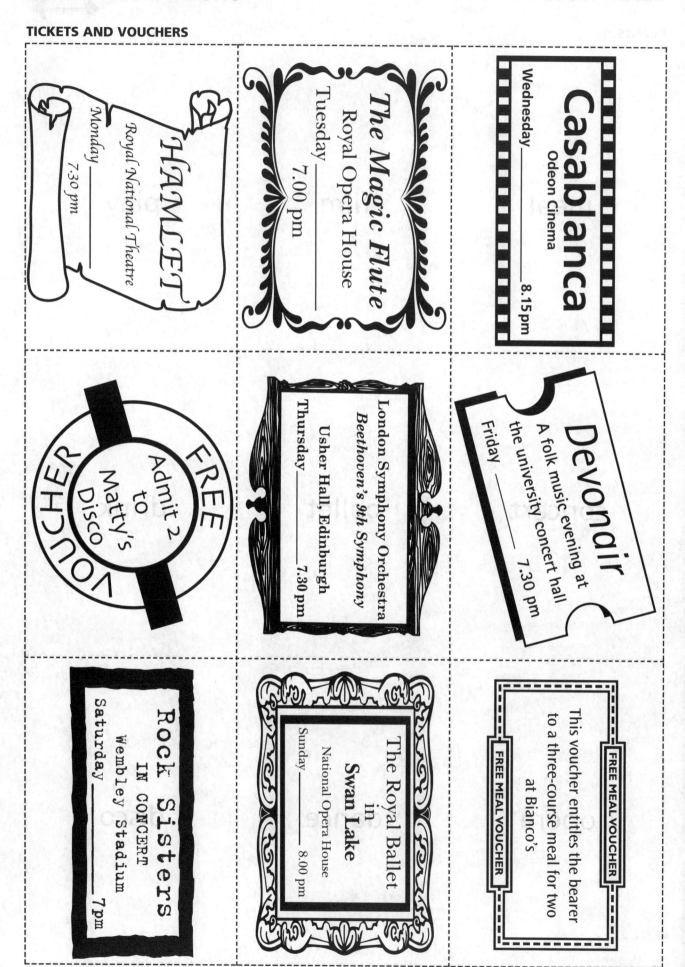

3 Restaurants

FOOD AND DRINK (1)

3 Restaurants

FOOD AND DRINK (1)

prawn cocktail	melon	avocado
lamb stew	beefsteak	vegetable soup
roast chicken	ham	pork chops
vegetarian pasta	stir-fried vegetables	grilled fish
boiled potatoes	roast potatoes	vegetable curry with rice
chips	jacket potato	mashed potatoes
cauliflower	carrots	peas

3 Restaurants

FOOD AND DRINK (2)

Intermediate Vocabulary Games
Pearson Education Limited   © J Hadfield 1999

3 Restaurants

FOOD AND DRINK (2)

salad	courgettes	green beans
cheesecake	chocolate mousse	ice cream
fruit	strawberry tart	apple pie
beer	cheese	yoghurt
sherry	gin and tonic	wine
brandy	whisky	cider
mineral water	orange juice	lemonade

3 Restaurants

MENU

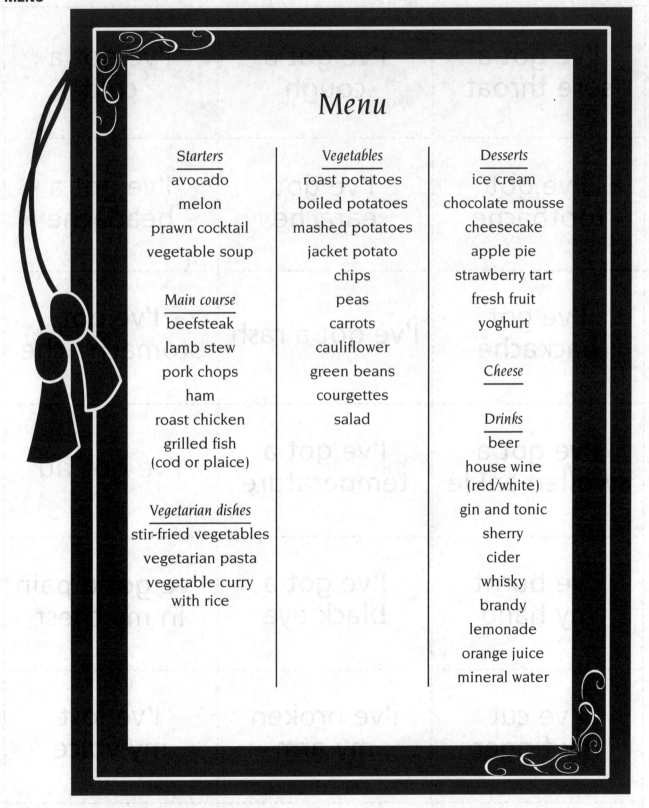

Menu

Starters
avocado
melon
prawn cocktail
vegetable soup

Main course
beefsteak
lamb stew
pork chops
ham
roast chicken
grilled fish
(cod or plaice)

Vegetarian dishes
stir-fried vegetables
vegetarian pasta
vegetable curry
with rice

Vegetables
roast potatoes
boiled potatoes
mashed potatoes
jacket potato
chips
peas
carrots
cauliflower
green beans
courgettes
salad

Desserts
ice cream
chocolate mousse
cheesecake
apple pie
strawberry tart
fresh fruit
yoghurt

Cheese

Drinks
beer
house wine
(red/white)
gin and tonic
sherry
cider
whisky
brandy
lemonade
orange juice
mineral water

4 Illness

AILMENTS WORDS

I've got a sore throat	I've got a cough	I've got a cold
I've got toothache	I've got earache	I've got a headache
I've got backache	I've got a rash	I've got stomach ache
I've got a swollen ankle	I've got a temperature	I've got flu
I've burnt my hand	I've got a black eye	I've got a pain in my chest
I've cut my finger	I've broken my arm	I've lost my voice
My knee hurts	I feel sick	I've sprained my wrist

4 Illness

AILMENTS PICTURES

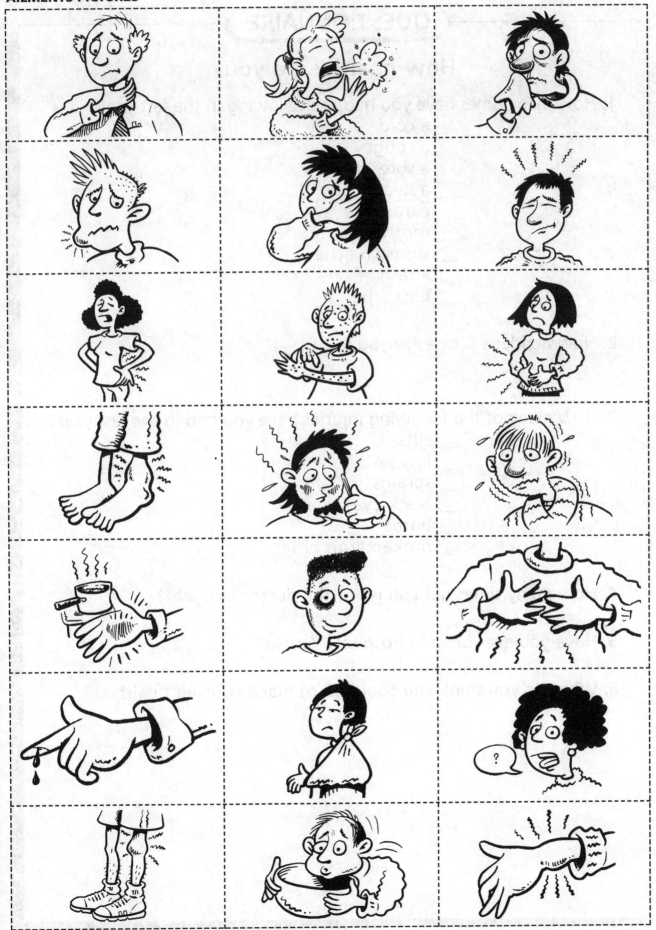

4 Illness

HEALTH QUESTIONNAIRE

QUESTIONNAIRE

How healthy are you?

1. How many times have you had the following in the last year?
___ a cold
___ a cough
___ a sore throat
___ a headache
___ earache
___ toothache
___ stomach ache
___ a rash
___ backache

2. How accident-prone are you?

3. How many of the following injuries have you had in the last year?
___ cuts
___ bruises
___ sprains
___ black eyes
___ burns
___ broken arms or legs

4. How many times did you go to the doctor last year? ___

5. Have you ever been in hospital? Yes/No

6. What do you think you could do to make yourself healthier?

4 Illness

REMEDIES

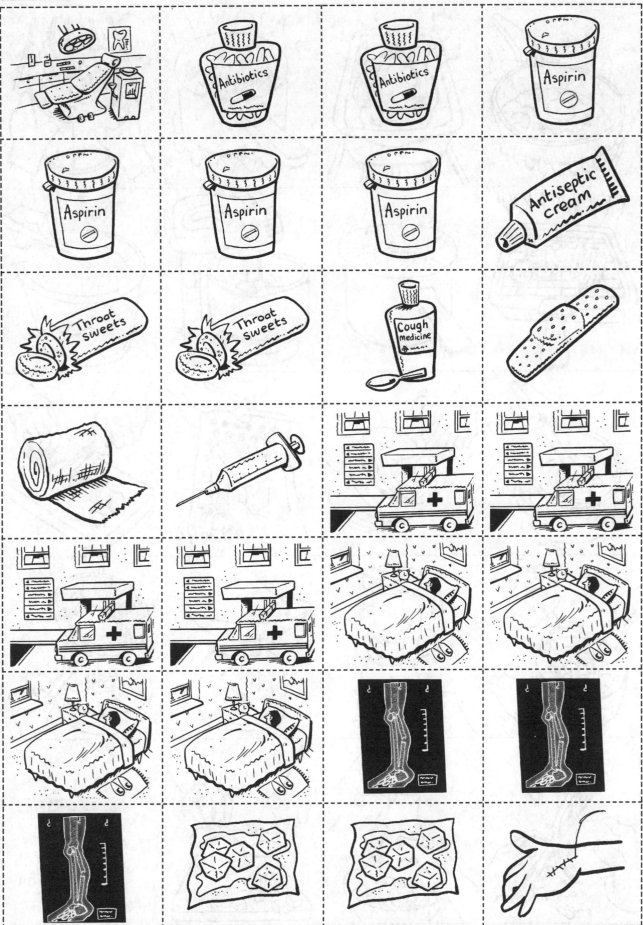

5 Cookery

COOKING

5 Cookery

COOKING

bake	boil	roast	fry
add	mix	simmer	grill
chop	grate	beat	stir
sieve	weigh	blend	mash
	dice	season	peel

5 Cookery

UTENSILS

1	scales	sieve	mixer	cake tin
2	knife	masher	wooden spoon	grill pan
3	peeler	knife	saucepan	blender
4	fork	grater	saltcellar, pepper mill	frying pan
	roasting tin	saucepan	spoon	whisk

5 Cookery

RECIPES

1 Cherry cake

Weigh 2 oz butter, 2 oz sugar and 4 oz cherries.

Weigh and sieve 4 oz flour.

Mix the ingredients together with two eggs.

Put the mixture in a greased cake tin and bake at 150 degrees centigrade for 30 minutes.

Remove from oven and turn out of tin when cool.

2 Potato cakes

Mash 1 lb boiled potatoes until smooth.

Dice one onion finely.

Stir the potato and onion together with an egg.

Make the mixture into small flat cakes and place under the grill.

Grill for ten minutes, turning once.

3 Pea and ham soup

Peel and chop two large carrots.

Put them in a saucepan with a ham bone, 8 oz dried peas and 2 pints of water.

Simmer for 1 to 2 hours.

Remove the ham bone and put the liquid in a blender.

Blend the liquid until smooth, then return to the saucepan and reheat.

4 Cheese omelette

Take 2 eggs and beat them.

Grate 2 oz cheese.

Heat 1 oz butter in a frying pan.

When hot, pour in the eggs, and season.

Fry until the eggs are just solid, then sprinkle the cheese on top.

When the cheese is melted, slide the omelette out of the pan onto a plate.

6 Animals

ANIMALS WORDS

cat	dog	goldfish	tortoise
parrot	rabbit	lion	tiger
mouse	duck	hippo	elephant
rhino	crocodile	frog	hen (chicken)
snake	zebra	sheep	cow
camel	bear	horse	pig
kangaroo	hamster	canary	guinea pig
seal	goat	goose	

6 Animals

ANIMALS PICTURES / LOTTO BOARDS

7 School and university subjects

BOOKS

TIMETABLE

	Monday	Tuesday	Wednesday	Thursday	Friday
9.00	MATHS	FRENCH	MATHS	FRENCH	MATHS
10.00	ENGLISH	HISTORY	ENGLISH	PSYCHOLOGY	ENGLISH
11.00	GERMAN	GEOGRAPHY	GERMAN	GEOGRAPHY	MUSIC
12.00	PHYSICS	BIOLOGY	CHEMISTRY	PHYSICS	BIOLOGY
2.00	CHEMISTRY	THEOLOGY	P.E.	PHILOSOPHY	POLITICS
3.00	DRAMA	LITERATURE	P.E.	LITERATURE	ART

7 School and university subjects

BOOKS: SUBJECTS

Music	Geography	History
Chemistry	Biology	Physics
Physical education (P.E.)	Theology/ Religious education	Maths
Politics	Psychology	Philosophy
	Literature	Drama

7 School and university subjects

LIBRARY PLAN

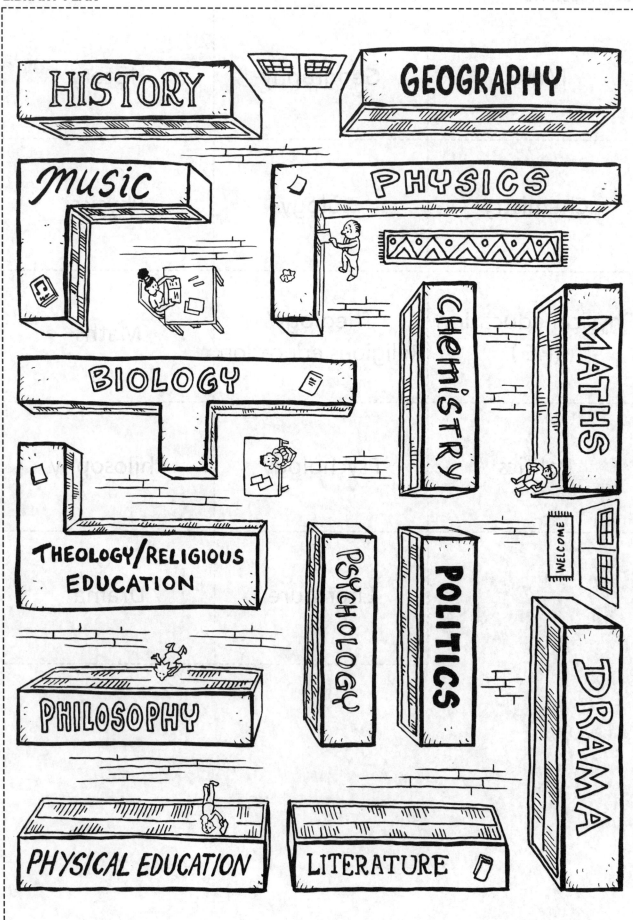

7 School and university subjects

HALL OF RESIDENCE PLAN

7 School and university subjects

REGISTRATION FORMS

 UNIVERSITY of DOVER
STUDENT REGISTRATION FORM

NAME: John Black

DATE OF BIRTH: 13.3.1981

YEAR: One

SUBJECT: History

 UNIVERSITY of DOVER
STUDENT REGISTRATION FORM

NAME: Lisa Jarvis

DATE OF BIRTH: 18.10.1978

YEAR: Three

SUBJECT: Chemistry

 UNIVERSITY of DOVER
STUDENT REGISTRATION FORM

NAME: Amy Davies

DATE OF BIRTH: 22.8.1980

YEAR: Two

SUBJECT: Psychology

 UNIVERSITY of DOVER
STUDENT REGISTRATION FORM

NAME: Sarah Brown

DATE OF BIRTH: 17.2.1980

YEAR: Two

SUBJECT: Geography

 UNIVERSITY of DOVER
STUDENT REGISTRATION FORM

NAME: Simon Boot

DATE OF BIRTH: 26.4.1981

YEAR: One

SUBJECT: Maths

 UNIVERSITY of DOVER
STUDENT REGISTRATION FORM

NAME: Pooran Singh

DATE OF BIRTH: 14.9.1979

YEAR: Three

SUBJECT: Politics

 UNIVERSITY of DOVER
STUDENT REGISTRATION FORM

NAME: Hussein Ali

DATE OF BIRTH: 21.5.1979

YEAR: Three

SUBJECT: Music

 UNIVERSITY of DOVER
STUDENT REGISTRATION FORM

NAME: Mary Tang

DATE OF BIRTH: 30.3.1980

YEAR: Two

SUBJECT: Theology

 UNIVERSITY of DOVER
STUDENT REGISTRATION FORM

NAME: Kirsten McDonald

DATE OF BIRTH: 12.1.1981

YEAR: One

SUBJECT: Drama

 UNIVERSITY of DOVER
STUDENT REGISTRATION FORM

NAME: Caroline Jones

DATE OF BIRTH: 25.11.1980

YEAR: One

SUBJECT: Physics

 UNIVERSITY of DOVER
STUDENT REGISTRATION FORM

NAME: Trevor Hollifield

DATE OF BIRTH: 18.6.1979

YEAR: Three

SUBJECT: Physical education

 UNIVERSITY of DOVER
STUDENT REGISTRATION FORM

NAME: Gwyneth Jones

DATE OF BIRTH: 7.2.1980

YEAR: Two

SUBJECT: Literature

 UNIVERSITY of DOVER
STUDENT REGISTRATION FORM

NAME: Patrick Stapleton

DATE OF BIRTH: 13.12.1979

YEAR: Two

SUBJECT: Biology

 UNIVERSITY of DOVER
STUDENT REGISTRATION FORM

NAME: Luke Collins

DATE OF BIRTH: 10.7.1981

YEAR: One

SUBJECT: Philosophy

 UNIVERSITY of DOVER
STUDENT REGISTRATION FORM

NAME: Carla Martinez

DATE OF BIRTH: 6.8.1979

YEAR: Three

SUBJECT: Art

8 Sports

SPORTS WORDS

shuttlecock	running shoes	slopes	opponent
stumps	hurdle	court	referee
cap	pole	pitch	umpire
tee	boots	golf course	game
hockey stick	sticks	track	match
bat	racquet	rink	round
ball	golf club	team	tournament
skates	net	players	championship
skis	goal	competitors	cup

8 Sports

ADDITIONAL WORDS

ball	ball	diamond	goal
ball	racquet	field	goal
ball	bat	court	net
ball	pitch	boots	hockey stick

QUIZ

Question: How many players are there in a baseball team?
Answer: Nine

Question: Name **two** sports that need bats.
Answer: cricket, baseball

Question: Name **two** pieces of equipment you need to play golf.
Answer: e.g. club, ball, tee

Question: Which **two** sports have eleven players in a team?
Answer: football, cricket

Question: Name **two** sports that need racquets.
Answer: tennis, badminton

Question: Name **one** sport played on a court and **one** sport played on a pitch.
Answer: court - e.g. tennis, badminton; pitch - e.g. football, cricket

Question: Name **two** sports that have nets.
Answer: tennis, badminton

Question: Which sport uses a shuttlecock?
Answer: badminton

Question: Name **two** sports that have goals.
Answer: e.g. hockey, ice hockey, football

Question: Name **two** sports that are played against one opponent only.
Answer: tennis, golf

8 Sports

SPORTS PICTURES

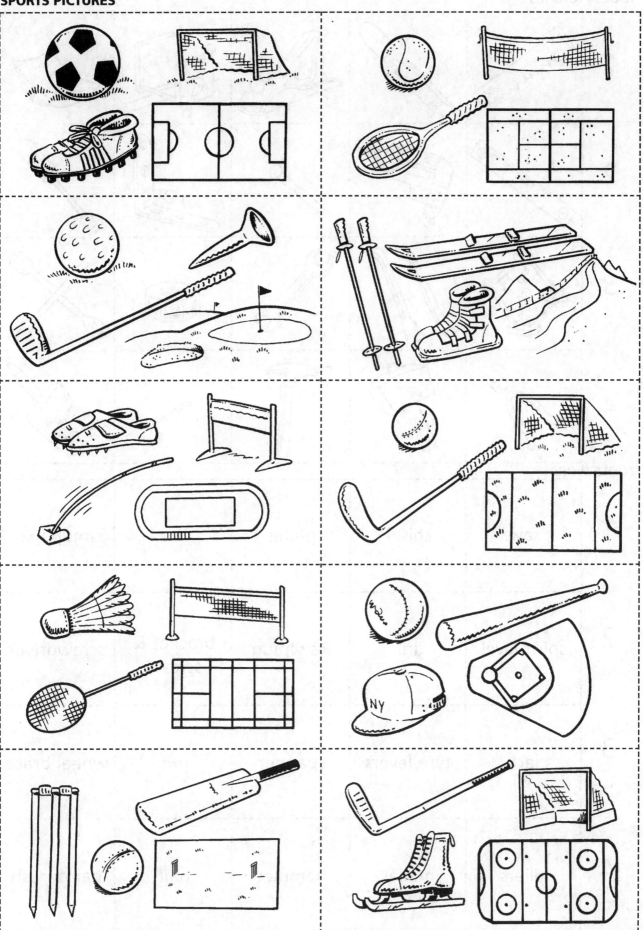

9 Tools and DIY

TOOLS PICTURES

1				
2				
3				
4				

TOOLS WORDS

1	saw	chisel	plane	vice	sandpaper
2	spirit level	drill	Rawlplug	bracket & screws	screwdriver
3	jack	tyre levers	spanner	nut	wheel brace
4	pliers	mallet	hammer	nail	paintbrush

9 Tools and DIY

HOUSEHOLD JOBS

1 Make a box

2 Put the shelf up

3 Change the tyre

4 Mend the fence

10 Office objects

OFFICE PICTURE

LABELS

desk	telephone	in-tray	mobile phone	out-tray
computer	fax machine	wastepaper bin	answering machine	telephone directories
stapler	printer	calculator	memo pad	stationery cupboard
filing cabinet	swivel chair	diary	photocopier	desk lamp
files	paperclip	calendar	mouse mat	hole punch

ANSWERS: 1 desk **2** computer **3** stapler **4** filing cabinet **5** files **6** telephone **7** fax machine **8** printer
9 swivel chair **10** paperclip **11** in-tray **12** wastepaper bin **13** calculator **14** diary **15** calendar **16** mobile phone
17 answering machine **18** memo pad **19** photocopier **20** mouse mat **21** out-tray **22** telephone directories
23 stationery cupboard **24** desk lamp **25** hole punch

10 Office objects

UNTIDY OFFICE A

10 Office objects

UNTIDY OFFICE B

11 Computers

HARDWARE

HARDWARE WORDS

screen	mouse	laptop	CD-ROM drive
monitor / VDU	printer	hard disk	cable
keyboard	scanner	floppy disk	modem

11 Computers

SOFTWARE WORDS

Internet	word processing	database	e-mail / email
web site / website	spreadsheet	graphics	program
World Wide Web			

			1	typing documents such as letters or reports

SOFTWARE DEFINITIONS

2 a program used to display numbers and other information in a grid	3 a program which can store and allow manipulation of a large amount of information	4 computer pictures and images	5 a system of sending messages between computers through the phone network, to specific addresses
6 the system that connects computers through telephone lines all over the world	7 Internet sites, containing text, graphics and sound, with links to each other	8 web pages published on the Internet by a person or organisation	9 a set of coded instructions, written in a programming language

ICONS AND COMMANDS

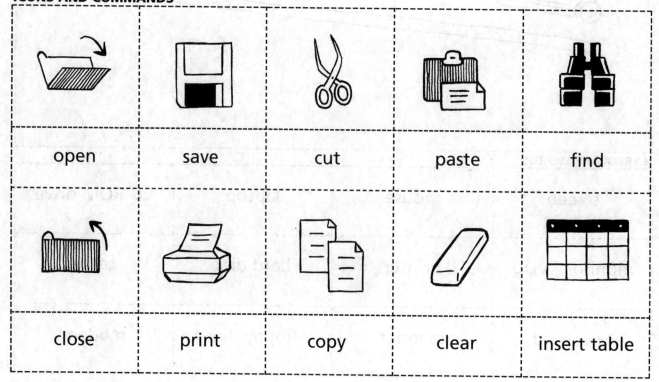

open	save	cut	paste	find
close	print	copy	clear	insert table

11 Computers

COLLOCATION

click	download	scan in	install
pull down	visit	print out	scroll down
a mouse	information	a document	a program
a menu	a web site / website	a file	a page

QUESTIONNAIRE

QUESTIONNAIRE

1. Choose one word or phrase to describe what you feel about computers:

   useful / fascinating / a waste of time / difficult to use

2. Do you have a computer at home?

3. Do you use one at work?

4. Which of the following do you know how to do?

   use a mouse
   pull down a menu
   print out a document
   use an image scanner
   use a CD-ROM
   get information on the Internet
   download information from the Internet
   send an e-mail
   use graphics
   use a database
   use spreadsheets

5. In your home, what is your computer used for most?

6. What would *you* use a computer for most?

   playing computer games
   educational CD-ROMs
   surfing the Internet
   sending e-mail
   word processing
   working with spreadsheets
   working with databases
   creating graphics

11 Computers

TROUBLESHOOTING: Problems

1 The computer is turned on but the screen is dark.

3 Typing on the keyboard produces nothing on the screen.

5 I've deleted a file by mistake.

7 The cursor suddenly stops moving.

2 The mouse won't move the cursor on the screen.

4 I can't save anything onto a floppy disk.

6 The printer won't print my document.

8 A message saying 'System Error' has appeared on the screen.

TROUBLESHOOTING: Solutions

1 Check that the monitor is switched on, or check the brightness control and turn it up.

3 Check that the keyboard cable is connected to the computer.

5 Double-click the Recycle Bin icon on the desktop. Select the file. Click on the File menu, then click Restore.

7 There is a software problem. Press Ctrl + Alt + Delete, then End Task to close the program and then try to move the cursor. If this doesn't work, turn off the computer and wait 10 seconds before turning it on again.

2 Check that the mouse is connected properly. If it is disconnected, plug it in and restart your computer.

4 The disk may be full or damaged. Try another disk.

6 Check that the printer is turned on and connected properly.

8 There is a system problem. Try turning the computer off and on again. If the error message still appears, you will have to install the program all over again or get expert help.

12 Actions (1)

ACTIONS

waving	rushing	stealing
holding	arguing	pointing
pressing	hopping	yawning
grinning	chatting	hitting
shouting	hugging	shaking
whispering	twisting	tugging
tripping	grabbing	smiling

QUESTIONNAIRE

QUESTIONNAIRE

When was the last time you did these things?

1. shake hands (with whom?) _____

2. yawn (why?) _____

3. rush to get somewhere (where? why?) _____

4. whisper something (what?) _____

5. argue (about what?) _____

6. have a good chat (who with?) _____

7. shout (what?) _____

8. hug someone (who?) _____

9. smile (at whom?) _____

12 Actions (1)

STREET SCENE A

STREET SCENE B

13 Actions (2)

ADVERBS

quietly	quickly	carefully	bravely
loudly	angrily	carelessly	joyfully
sadly	calmly	aggressively	gloomily
happily	impatiently	gently	nervously
slowly	patiently	timidly	confidently

QUESTIONNAIRE

QUESTIONNAIRE

Think of something real or imaginary you did last week:

- happily
- quietly
- quickly
- carefully
- nervously
- impatiently
- calmly
- gently
- slowly
- loudly

Write the sentences, e.g.

My friend phoned me and we talked happily for over an hour!

I found an injured bird in the garden. I put it carefully in a box and took it to the vet.

13 Actions (2)

GENTLY DOES IT

How would you shut …

How would you talk to …

How would you walk …

How would you sing …

How would you talk to …

How would you read …

How would you tell …

How would you write …

How would you wait …

How would you open …

How would you speak …

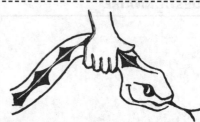

How would you pick up …

How would you run …

How would you wait …

How would you open …

How would you carry …

How would you stroke …

How would you open …

14 Approval and disapproval

ADJECTIVES

good	terrific	okay	disgusting
nice	sweet	all right / alright	dreadful
brilliant	cute	not bad	ridiculous
fantastic	super	so-so	vile
wonderful	lovely	awful	nasty
amazing	marvellous	terrible	boring
great	excellent	horrible	horrific

15 People

APPEARANCE

short	plump	beautiful	ugly	neatly dressed
tall	well built	attractive	smartly dressed	anxious-looking
tall	skinny	pretty	well dressed	happy-looking
medium height	slim	handsome	elegantly dressed	angry-looking
overweight	thin	good-looking	casually dressed	sad-looking
tubby	muscular	plain	scruffily dressed	tired-looking

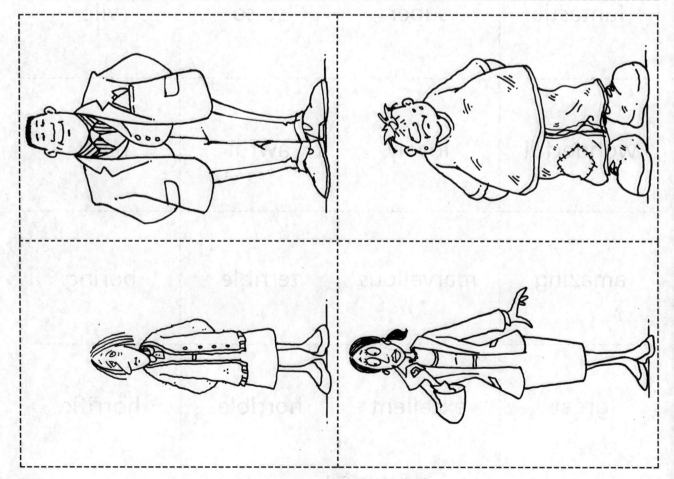

15 People

FACE AND HEAD

bald	short hair	white hair	square face	thick lips	slanting eyes
straight hair	fair hair	grey hair	round face	thin lips	almond eyes
wavy hair	black hair	long nose	oval face	thin lips	pointed chin
curly hair	brown hair	hooked nose	heart-shaped face	round eyes	pointed chin
blonde hair	long hair	snub nose	long face	round eyes	double chin
red hair	dark hair	broad nose	full lips	short hair	double chin

15 People

DREAM ROMANCE

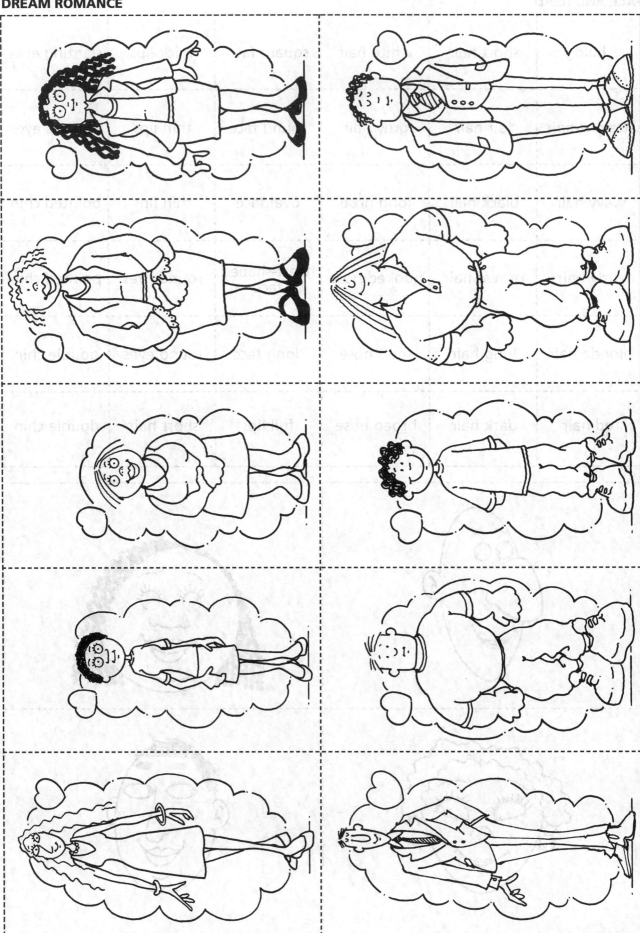

15 People

AVAILABLE PARTNERS

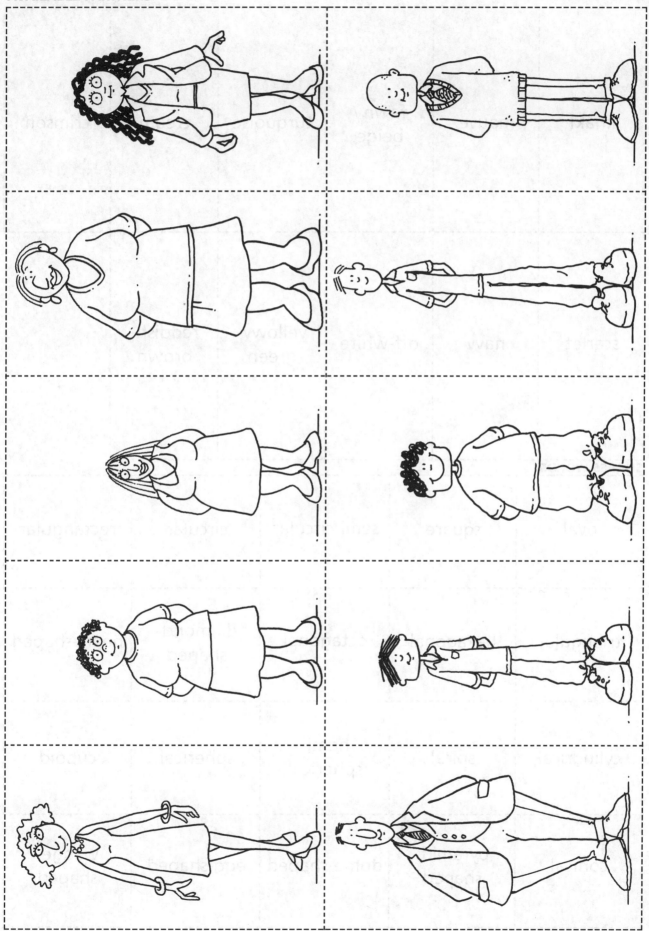

16 Colours and shapes

COLOURS

khaki	mauve	fawn / beige	turquoise	cream	crimson
scarlet	navy	off-white	yellowy-green	reddish-brown	

SHAPES WORDS

oval	square	semi-circular	circular	rectangular
triangular	hexagonal	octagonal	diamond-shaped	heart-shaped
cylindrical	spiral	hemi-spherical	spherical	cuboid
conical	pyramid-shaped	dome-shaped	egg-shaped	wedge-shaped

16 Colours and shapes

SHAPES PICTURES

OPPOSITE FORMS

hollow	solid	sharp	blunt	pointed	rounded
concave	convex	straight	bent	straight	crooked
straight	curved	smooth	rough	smooth	jagged

16 Colours and shapes

PLANET ZARG

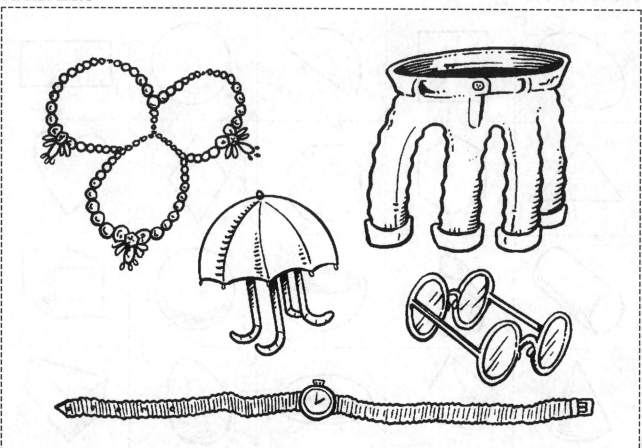

PLANET THARG

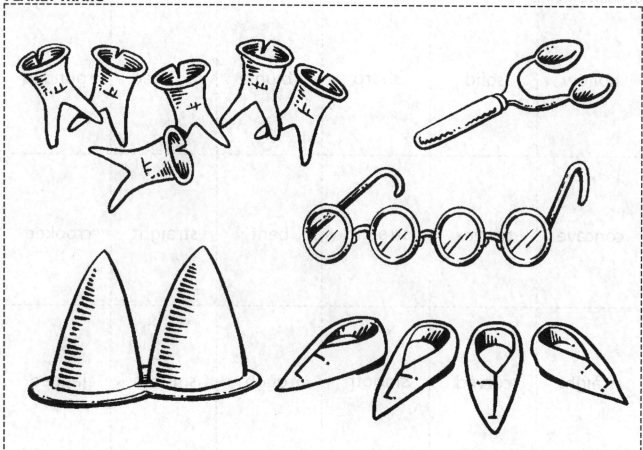

17 Scenery

LANDSCAPES PICTURES

17 Scenery

LANDSCAPES WORDS

farmland	desert	jungle / rain forest	forest	woodland
hills	grassland	pasture	moorland	mountain range
swamp	canyon	bush		

TERRAINS

a flat, barren landscape	a level, grassy plain	rich, rolling farmland	gently sloping, lush green meadows	steep hills
a mountainous landscape	densely forested hills	thickly wooded hills	a wide plain, sparsely dotted with trees	a wild and craggy landscape
a barren, rocky landscape	marshy ground	tangled undergrowth		

17 Scenery

ATMOSPHERES

dramatic	majestic	gloomy	lonely
peaceful	monotonous	gentle	desolate
mysterious	exciting	awe-inspiring	romantic

WILDLIFE

cow	camel	monkey	squirrel
sheep	goat	horse	rabbit
alligator	lizard	lion	chamois
parrot	racoon	antelope	frog

18 Sounds

NOISES

whistle	bang	click	thump
hum	howl	cry	rumble
scream	roar	growl	tick
chirp	pop	rattle	rustle
squeak	creak	buzz	splash

18 Sounds

SOUNDS PICTURES

19 Sensations

OBJECTS (1)

19 Sensations

OBJECTS (1)

dry	wet	heavy	light
hot	cold	foul-smelling	fragrant
soft	hard	smooth	rough
salty	bitter	sour	sweet
furry	prickly	bland / tasteless	spicy
hairy	greasy	slimy	slippery

19 Sensations

OBJECTS (2)

20 Emotions

EMOTIONS PICTURES / LOTTO BOARDS

happy	sad	surprised	frightened
worried	angry	nervous	impatient
proud	disappointed	curious	embarrassed
hurt	jealous	shocked	relieved
grateful	puzzled		

delighted	fed up

20 Emotions

SITUATIONS

21 Personality

PERSONALITIES

calm	emotional	funny	serious
gentle	rough	kind	unkind
generous	mean	polite	rude
good-tempered	bad-tempered	sociable	shy
confident	nervous	adventurous	domestic
miserable	jolly	decisive	indecisive

21 Personality

JOBS

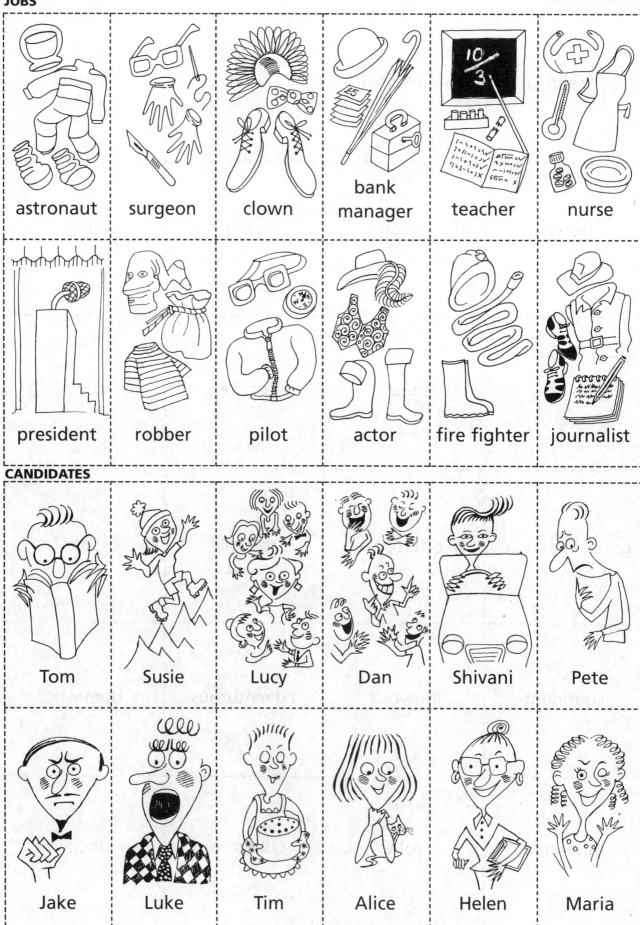

astronaut · surgeon · clown · bank manager · teacher · nurse

president · robber · pilot · actor · fire fighter · journalist

CANDIDATES

Tom · Susie · Lucy · Dan · Shivani · Pete

Jake · Luke · Tim · Alice · Helen · Maria

22 Travel

TRAVEL WORDS

ticket	passport	money	traveller's cheques	foreign currency
guidebook	visa	platform	waiting room	departure lounge
departure bay	departure gate/boarding gate	station	airport	ferry terminal
coach station	passenger	guard	ticket collector	customs official
pilot	stewardess	driver	captain	crew
bursar	passport control	customs	ticket desk	check in
driver	crew	ticket collector	captain	waiting room
departure lounge	customs official	passenger	passenger	passenger

TOKENS

22 Travel

JOURNEYS

COACH

1 COACH STATION

You've got to the coach station. But you forgot your money! Go home to get it. Then throw a five to get to the **ticket desk.**

2 TICKET DESK

You're lucky, there is no queue and you can get your ticket quickly. Go straight to the **waiting room.**

3 WAITING ROOM

Sorry! You've just missed your coach. Go back to the **information desk** to find out when there'll be another coach.

4 INFORMATION DESK

There isn't another coach for two hours! Go to the **waiting room. Miss a go,** then throw a three to get to the **departure bay.**

5 DEPARTURE BAY

The coach is there, the passengers are there, but where's the driver? **Miss a go** while he has his tea! Then throw a four to get on the **coach.**

6 COACH

Congratulations – you've finally got on the coach! And so has the driver! But the traffic is heavy: throw a four to DEPART.

FERRY

1 FERRY TERMINAL

You've got to the ferry terminal. Go straight to the **check in** desk to show your ticket.

2 CHECK IN

Now you realise you left your ticket at home. Take a taxi home to find it. **Miss a go.** Then throw a three to get to the **ferry terminal** again. When you reach the terminal, go straight to **check in**. Then throw a four to get to **passport control.**

3 PASSPORT CONTROL

There's no queue. Go straight through to **customs and baggage check.**

4 CUSTOMS and BAGGAGE CHECK

For some reason the customs officials decide to search your luggage! **Miss a go.** Then throw a four to get to the **departure lounge.**

5 DEPARTURE LOUNGE

At last! You're ready to embark. No time to wait, though – the ferry is about to sail. Go straight to **embarkation!**

6 EMBARKATION

You've just made it! The ship is ready to leave. But the sea is rough: throw a two to DEPART.

PLANE

1 AIRPORT

You've got to the airport in good time. Well done! Go straight to the **check in.**

2 CHECK IN

There is a long queue. **Miss a go** while you wait. Then throw a five to get to **passport control.**

3 PASSPORT CONTROL

You're waiting here when you suddenly realise you have forgotten to change any money. **Miss a go** while you search for a bureau de change. Then throw a three to get to **customs and baggage check.**

4 CUSTOMS and BAGGAGE CHECK

At the baggage check they are searching everyone's hand luggage. Throw a four to get to the **departure lounge.**

5 DEPARTURE LOUNGE

Your flight is being called! No time to buy anything in the shops! Go straight to the **boarding gate!**

6 BOARDING GATE

Congratulations! You're on your way. There is a short delay while the pilot waits for a runway: throw a one before you can DEPART.

TRAIN

1 STATION

You're at the station. Your journey is about to begin. Go to the **ticket desk.**

2 TICKET DESK

There is a man at the front of the queue with a very complicated query. He is holding everyone up. **Miss a go** while you wait. Then throw a six to get to the **waiting room.**

3 WAITING ROOM

At last! You've got your ticket. But you hear an announcement that your train has been cancelled. Go back to the **information desk** to find out the time of the next train.

4 INFORMATION DESK

There isn't another train for an hour. Go to the **waiting room** again. **Miss a go.** Then throw a six to get to the **platform.**

5 PLATFORM

You're on the platform, but there's no sign of the train. You hear an announcement that it's half an hour late because of signal failures. Throw a four before you can get on the **train.**

6 TRAIN

Congratulations! You can get on the train at last. But it isn't moving: throw a three to DEPART.

22 Travel

MISSED CONNECTIONS

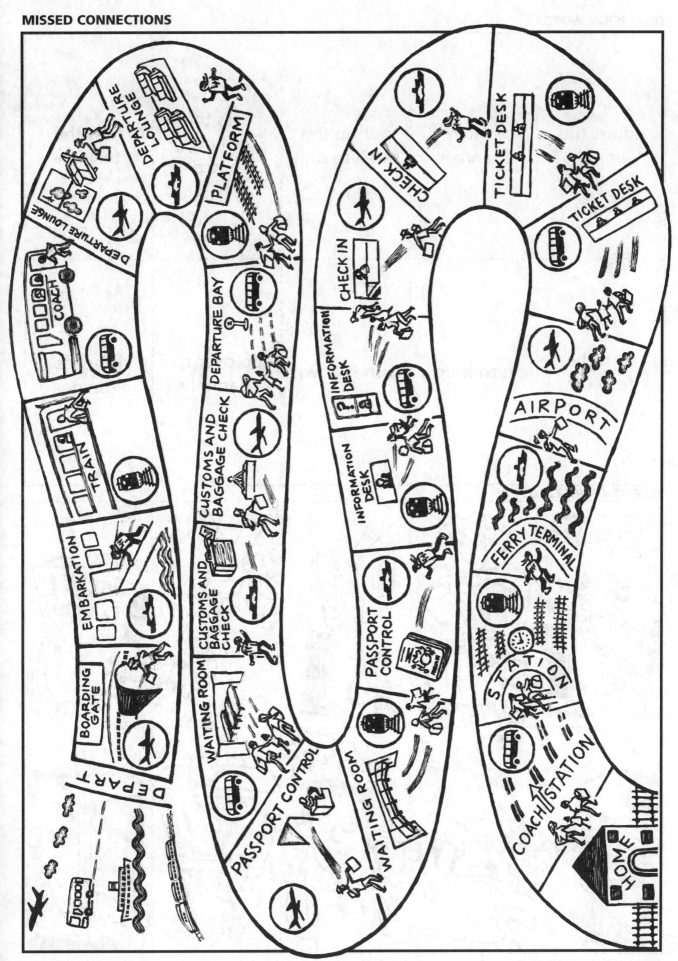

23 Television

TELEVISION WORDS

adjust the aerial	switch channels	put up the satellite dish	pass the remote control	turn the telly on
turn the telly off	turn it up	turn it down	go over to Channel 4	it needs tuning

TELEVISION PICTURES

23 Television

PROGRAMME TYPES

sitcom	drama	documentary	fly-on-the-wall documentary / docu-soap
comedy show	cookery programme	health programme	chat show
news programme	soap (opera)	sports programme	current affairs programme
game show	quiz show	cartoon	film / movie
interview	arts programme	music programme	serial
wildlife programme	travel programme	children's programme	magazine programme

OPINIONS

interesting	stimulating	boring	rubbish
funny	gripping	exciting	trivial

23 Television

PROGRAMMES

Channel 1	Channel 2	Channel 3	Channel 4
6.00 Carnation Street In this episode Tracey is suspicious of Mark's behaviour while an incident in the pub shocks Kevin.	**6.00 Sharp Practice** The medical drama serial continues with the first of a two-part story.	**6.00 Our Working Lives** First of a four-part documentary series looking at the lives of workers in modern Britain.	**6.00 Children's TV** Tellybellies The Tellybellies meet two children whose father is a zoo keeper.
6.30 Health Matters The weekly health magazine, presented by Dr Tim Blakeney. Tonight's edition looks at the bone disease osteoporosis.	**6.30 Sabrina** Live weekday chat show hosted by Sabrina Simms.	**6.30 Comment** A report on the Northern Ireland peace process.	**6.30 Goal!** This week's best goals from the matches.
7.00 Here's Trouble Comedy starring Adam Redstart. Adam invites top executives to visit his factory.	**7.30 News and Views** Presented by Jeremy Flashman.	**7.30 Top Brain** General knowledge quiz show.	**7.30 The Little Tiger Cub** Animated cartoon tale of life in an Indian jungle.
8.30 The Purple Saxifrage Last of three dramas based on Countess Orlovsky's classic tales, starring Richard Kennedy and Elizabeth Shaw. The heir to the Austrian throne is being kidnapped. Can the Purple Saxifrage save him?	**8.30 Hi!** Weekday magazine with Pam Smith and Felix Featherstone. Including news and weather on the hour and half hour. Featuring an interview with actress Jenny Lovegrove, who discusses her latest film *The Heart Thief*.	**8.30 A and E** In tonight's report from the Accident and Emergency department at Tom Paine Hospital, the trauma team attempt to save the life of a rock climber.	**8.30 Talking Sense** with Angus Stewart Interviews with newsmakers.
9.30 In the Sun Terry Makepeace presents reports on the holiday destinations of Hawaii and Florida.	**9.30 Amanda Nichols** A profile of violinist Amanda Nichols whose passionate style of playing has won her international acclaim.	**9.30 BLOTTO** Game show with Tom Bunkhouse.	**9.30 Pop** Continuing the comedy about a father-and-son household. Everything seems to be going well for Tony until Pop turns up with a new girlfriend.
10.00 What's Cooking? Ways with chocolate. Jane Fisher uses chocolate in the first of five inventive recipes.	**10.00 Animal Kingdom** Continuing the feature on the chimps of Gombe National Park in Tanzania.	**10.00 Life at Giverny** Last in the series on lives of the Impressionist artists, this programme looks at domestic life in the Monet household.	**10.00 My Goldfish is an Alien** Sci-fi film about an alien from the far-off planet Serena who is sent to spy on life on Earth in the form of a goldfish. Things get complicated when he falls in love with his beautiful owner and tries to break out of his bowl.

23 Television

FAMILY ROLES

GRANDMA
like
soaps, sitcoms, docu-soaps
don't like
serious programmes like news or current affairs

DAD
like
comedy shows, chat shows, docu-soaps
don't like
serious programmes like news or current affairs

MARY
like
comedy shows, sitcoms, cookery programmes
don't like
serious programmes like news or current affairs

GRANDPA
like
documentaries, news, current affairs
don't like
soaps, chat shows, sitcoms

MUM
like
documentaries, interviews, arts programmes
don't like
soaps, chat shows, sitcoms

TOM
like
arts, music and current affairs
don't like
soaps, chat shows, sitcoms

AUNTIE SUSAN
like
comedy shows, chat shows, docu-soaps
don't like
serious programmes like news or current affairs

SARAH
like
comedy shows, sitcoms, cookery programmes
don't like
serious programmes like news or current affairs

UNCLE MIKE
like
documentaries, news, current affairs
don't like
soaps, chat shows, sitcoms

ANNA
like
documentaries, interviews, arts programmes
don't like
soaps, chat shows, sitcoms

ALEX
like
arts, music and current affairs
don't like
soaps, chat shows, sitcoms

24 Holidays

HOLIDAY TYPES

skiing holiday	camping holiday	caravanning holiday
safari	seaside holiday	beach holiday
hiking holiday	cycling holiday	coach tour
cruise	self-catering holiday (in an apartment or villa)	hotel holiday

ACTIVITIES

sunbathing	sightseeing	buying souvenirs
exploring	sailing	surfing
windsurfing	snorkelling	trying the local food
going to bars and discos	getting fresh air and exercise	meeting people and learning about other cultures

24 Holidays

POSTCARDS

24 Holidays

CLICHÉS

So peaceful and romantic!	It's good to get off the beaten track, away from it all.	The town is very lively, quite touristy, the nightlife's good, though!
Enjoying sightseeing in this picturesque old town.	**Having a thrilling time - a real adventure.**	Greetings from Paradise - we won't want to leave this idyllic place ...
Enjoying the fresh air and exercise — and the stunning scenery!	Having a great time just relaxing.	*Enjoying the outdoor life and freedom.*
Great sun and snow, glorious mountain scenery. Après ski is good too!	The apartment is noisy, nothing works, we'll be glad to get home.	**Unfortunately the site is very crowded and the local people aren't very friendly.**

HOLIDAYMAKERS

You want: Somewhere peaceful and relaxing. No price limit.	**You want:** Adventure and excitement. Price limit: under £1000.	**You want:** An outdoor holiday. Price limit: £250.
You want: An activity holiday with opportunities for sports. Price limit: £500.	**You want:** Somewhere exotic and idyllic. Price limit: about £800.	**You want:** A beach holiday – somewhere lively with good nightlife. Price limit: around £300.
You want: Somewhere picturesque, with a lot of history and culture. Price limit: around £500.	**You want:** Somewhere not too touristy, off the beaten track. Price limit: up to £800.	**You want:** to be in the mountains. Price limit: up to £800, preferably less.

24 Holidays

TRAVEL AGENTS A

1 Mediterranean cruise!

Seven days on board the SS *Santa Maria*, visiting Malta, Italy, Sicily and Greece.

£1000 *Only 1 place remaining!*

2 Safari in Kenya

Five days in Masai Mara national park followed by a weekend at the coast at Mombasa.

£700 *Only 1 place remaining!*

3 Camp Italy!

Ready-erected tents in stunning locations: Dolomites, Tuscany, Sorrento.

£250 *Only 1 place remaining!*

4 Watersports in Tunisia

Half-board accommodation in four-star hotel. Opportunities for sailing, windsurfing and scuba diving.

£450 *Only 1 place remaining!*

5 A week in paradise

Beach bungalows in the tropical paradise of the Maldives.

£700 *Only 1 place remaining!*

6 Mikonos

Sophisticated Greek island resort. Wonderful scenery, great beaches, fantastic nightlife.

£300 *Only 1 place remaining!*

7 Trek Ladakh

Two weeks trekking in the Himalayas in this remote and fascinating country.

£800 *Only 1 place remaining!*

8 City break in Rome

Seven nights at the three-star Hotel Michelangelo.

£450 *Only 1 place remaining!*

TRAVEL AGENTS B

1 Barge holidays in France

Travel the French waterways on your own barge. Seven days on board.

£1000 per barge *Only 1 remaining!*

2 Trekking in Nepal

Two weeks trekking to Everest base camp. Basic accommodation in tea houses on the way.

£700 *Only 1 place remaining!*

3 Caravanning in France

Pre-book your sites in stunning locations: Provence, French Alps, south-west coast, Pyrenees.

£250 *Only 1 place remaining!*

4 One week's skiing in Courchevel

Self-catering studio accommodation.

£450 *Only 1 place remaining!*

5 A week in paradise

Beach bungalows in Thailand's tropical paradise, Phuket.

£700 *Only 1 place remaining!*

6 Costa del Sol, Spain

Lively resorts, long golden beaches, fantastic nightlife.

£300 *Only 1 place remaining!*

7 The Forbidden Kingdom of Bhutan

Two weeks' guided tour of this remote and fascinating country.

£800 *Only 1 place remaining!*

8 Beijing tour

Visit the Great Wall, the Ming Tombs and the Forbidden City.

£450 *Only 1 place remaining!*

TRAVEL AGENTS C

1 Stressed? Tired? Try our Stressbuster week!

Seven days on a health farm in a Scottish castle. You'll come away feeling like a king or queen!

£1000 *Only 1 place remaining!*

2 White-water rafting down the Zambesi river

Seven days rafting down one of the world's greatest rivers.

£700 *Only 1 place remaining!*

3 Cycle in Spain

A guided cycle tour in the Spanish Pyrenees.

£250 *Only 1 place remaining!*

4 Learn to sail in Greece

A week aboard our yacht, sailing round the Greek islands, will teach you the basics of sailing.

£450 *Only 1 place remaining!*

5 A week in paradise

Beach bungalows in the exotic tropical paradise of Bali.

£700 *Only 1 place remaining!*

6 Tenerife

Self-catering villas and apartments in Playa de las Americas. Wonderful scenery, great beaches, fantastic nightlife.

£300 *Only 1 place remaining!*

7 La Gomera - The unknown Canary Island

Walk, swim and sunbathe on this little-known but beautiful island.

£800 *Only 1 place remaining!*

8 Egypt adventure

Nile cruise, on luxury ship: visiting Pyramids and Luxor.

£450 *Only 1 place remaining!*

25 Work

ACTIVITIES

25 Work

ACTIVITIES

sign	sell	write reports	type / do word processing
be in charge of	interview	do the accounts	attend meetings
repair	meet clients	phone / answer phone calls	supervise / train
work on an assembly line / operate machinery	invoice	fit	install
draw up plans	research into / do research	invent / create	check
treat	diagnose	examine	design
deliver	collect	look after / care for	operate on

Intermediate Vocabulary Games
Pearson Education Limited © J Hadfield 1999

25 Work

CONDITIONS

1 salary	2 pay	3 income
4 regular hours	5 shift work	6 flexitime
7 full time	8 part time	9 jobshare
10 on nights / night shift	11 overtime	12 apply for
13 employer	14 employee	15 self-employed
16 trainee	17 apprentice	18 pay rise
19 salary increase	20 promotion	21 good prospects
22 job security	23 temporary job	24 permanent job
25 pension scheme	26 resign	27 get the sack
28 be fired	29 unemployed / out of work	30 retire

25 Work

CONDITIONS DEFINITIONS

money paid for doing a job	money paid for doing a job	money paid for doing a job
being able to choose or change the hours you work	working hours that vary from week to week	working at the same times each day
two people sharing one full-time job	working for only part of the week	working 35 hours a week or more
to try to get a job	doing work in addition to the normal hours	working during the night
working for yourself	person who is paid to work for someone else	person who pays others to work
an increase in the amount of money paid for doing a job	person who is being trained to do a job	person who is being trained to do a job
(good) possibilities for promotion	change or move to a more responsible or better-paid position	an increase in the amount of money paid for doing a job
a job for an unlimited length of time	a job with a contract for a limited time	having a job where you cannot easily be dismissed
to be told to leave a job	to leave a job (of your own free will)	you pay money each month in order to get an income when you retire
to finish your work for life	without a job	to be told to leave a job

25 Work

QUESTIONNAIRE

QUESTIONNAIRE

Imagine you are looking for a new job.
Which of the following are important to you?
Number them 1 to 3 in order of importance.
(1 = very important, 2 = quite important, 3 = not important)

- ☐ working with people
- ☐ working with information or ideas
- ☐ working with things
- ☐ a good salary
- ☐ a nine-to-five job with no shift work or night duty
- ☐ being able to work flexitime
- ☐ being able to work part-time
- ☐ being able to jobshare
- ☐ long holidays
- ☐ a good pension scheme
- ☐ regular pay rises
- ☐ job security
- ☐ good promotion prospects
- ☐ opportunities for early retirement

What is your ideal job?

25 Work

LOTTO

salesman	businesswoman
architect	secretary
surgeon	nurse
car mechanic	washing machine repair man
accountant	receptionist
fashion designer	postman
factory worker	scientist
vet	journalist

26 Crime

CRIMINALS

1 arsonist	**2** drug dealer	**3** vandal	**4** housebreaker
5 burglar	**6** hijacker	**7** mugger	**8** blackmailer
9 fraudster	**10** terrorist	**11** thief	**12** (armed) robber
13 murderer	**14** rapist	**15** shoplifter	**16** kidnapper
17 forger	**18** smuggler	**19** (football) hooligan	**20** assailant

DETECTION

arrest	trace	commit	detain
release	investigate	question	charge with

26 Crime

CRIMES

housebreaking	vandalism	drug dealing	arson
blackmail	mugging	hijacking	burglary
(armed) robbery	theft / stealing	bomb attack	fraud
kidnapping	shoplifting	rape	murder
assault	hooliganism	smuggling	forgery

26 Crime

MUGSHOTS

PRISON PLAN

26 Crime

INMATES

You are in cell 1. The man in the cell next to you hit a woman and stole her bag. Unfortunately for him, it contained only a bottle of milk and a baby's nappy.

You are in cell 2. On one side of you is a man who set fire to a fireworks factory. The police arrested him while he was watching the firework display.

On the other side is someone arrested for bringing gold bars into the country. The customs officials got suspicious when his trousers made a clanging noise as he walked.

You are in cell 3. On one side of you is a man who hit a woman and stole her bag. Unfortunately for him, it contained only a bottle of milk and a baby's nappy.

On the other side is someone arrested for forcing his way into a house to steal things. Unfortunately, it was a policeman's house and all his colleagues were there to celebrate his birthday.

You are in cell 4. On one side of you is someone arrested for bringing gold bars into the country. The customs officials got suspicious when his trousers made a clanging noise as he walked.

On the other side is someone who smashed up parked cars and painted graffiti all over them. Unfortunately, one of the cars was a police car and the graffiti he painted was his own name.

You are in cell 5. On one side of you is someone arrested for forcing his way into a house to steal things. Unfortunately, it was a policeman's house and all his colleagues were there to celebrate his birthday.

On the other side is someone who pointed a gun at the pilots of a plane and told them to take him to Bogotá. The plane was already going to Bogotá.

You are in cell 6. On one side of you is someone who smashed up parked cars and painted graffiti all over them. Unfortunately, one of the cars was a police car and the graffiti he painted was his own name.

On the other side is someone who threatened to tell his friend's wife that he was having an affair unless he gave him a lot of money. Unfortunately for him, the wife already knew and his friend told the police.

You are in cell 7. On one side of you is someone who pointed a gun at the pilots of a plane and told them to take him to Bogotá. The plane was already going to Bogotá.

On the other side is a man who planned to steal jewellery from a shop. Unfortunately, the phone rang when he was inside and he answered it, giving his own name.

You are in cell 8. On one side of you is someone who threatened to tell his friend's wife that he was having an affair unless he gave him a lot of money. Unfortunately for him, the wife already knew and his friend told the police.

On the other side is a man who went into a bank with a gun. Unfortunately, he tripped as he went down the steps – the money went all over the street and his gun went down a drain.

You are in cell 9. On one side of you is a man who planned to steal jewellery from a shop. Unfortunately the phone rang when he was inside and he answered it, giving his own name.

On the other side is a man who deceived people by selling cheap shirts with false designer labels. Unfortunately, he tried to sell some shirts to one of the designers.

You are in cell 10. On one side of you is a man who went into a bank with a gun. Unfortunately, he tripped as he went down the steps – the money went all over the street and his gun went down a drain.

On the other side is a man who went into a department store to steal a pair of shoes. Unfortunately, they were the wrong size and he was arrested when he went back to change them the next day.

You are in cell 11. On one side of you is a man who deceived people by selling cheap shirts with false designer labels. Unfortunately, he tried to sell some shirts to one of the designers.

On the other side is a man who tried to abduct a millionaire's son to ask for ransom money. He got the boy into his car, but unfortunately the car wouldn't start.

You are in cell 12. On one side of you is a man who went into a department store to steal a pair of shoes. Unfortunately, they were the wrong size and he was arrested when he went back to change them the next day.

On the other side is a man who tried to make his own bank notes. They looked very realistic, but unfortunately he couldn't spell, so the notes read: 'Twenty punds'.

You are in cell 13. On one side of you is a man who tried to abduct a millionaire's son to ask for ransom money. He got the boy into his car, but unfortunately the car wouldn't start.

On the other side is a man who got very drunk at a football match and attacked someone. Unfortunately, the person he picked a fight with was a champion boxer.

You are in cell 14. In the next cell to you is a man who tried to make his own bank notes. They looked very realistic, but unfortunately he couldn't spell, so the notes read: 'Twenty punds'.

27 The law

PROCEDURES

investigate a crime	arrest a suspect	make a statement
charge with a crime	be remanded in custody	be released on bail
brief a barrister	appear in court	be accused of (a crime / an offence)
plead innocent or guilty	be tried (for a crime / an offence)	give evidence
hear evidence	put the case for the prosecution	put the case for the defence
sum up	reach a verdict	pass a sentence

27 The law

PEOPLE

police officer

police officer

the defendant /
the accused

police officer

the defendant /
the accused

the defendant /
the accused

solicitor

the defendant /
the accused

the defendant /
the accused

the defendant /
the accused

the defendant /
the accused

witnesses

jury

counsel for the prosecution
(a barrister)

counsel for the
defence (a barrister)

judge

jury

judge

27 The law

COURTROOM SCENE

THE TRIAL OF RONNIE SMALLS

Ronnie Smalls: Defendant

You are a used-car salesman accused of stealing a car, a red Mosquito parked outside the owner's house last 25 April at 9.00 at night. You are in fact guilty of this offence – the mistake you made was to put an advert in the paper to sell the car. Only one person turned up to answer the ad. That would have been all right because he really wanted the car. The problem was, he was the car's original owner!

You don't know how to get out of this one – things look pretty bad! But you are good at looking innocent and you have some good mates who will stick up for you and swear you were with them at the time of the theft. So you intend to plead innocent. You're going to swear that someone sold you the car, and that you couldn't have taken it because you were at your mate Reggie's at the time.

Defending Counsel

The defendant, Ronnie Smalls, a used-car salesman, is accused of stealing a car, a red Mosquito parked outside the owner's house last 25 April at 9.00 at night. The mistake he made was to put an advert in the paper to sell the car. Only one person turned up to answer the ad – the car's original owner! But things aren't clear-cut. There are two witnesses who claim to have seen him driving the car, but there are three who have contradictory evidence. An interesting case!

You will be able to ask questions of all the witnesses. Ask for as many details as you like.

Prosecuting Counsel

The defendant, Ronnie Smalls, a used-car salesman, is accused of stealing a car, a red Mosquito parked outside the owner's house last 25 April at 9.00 at night. It seems a pretty clear-cut case to you – the mistake he made was to put an advert in the paper to sell the car. Only one person turned up to answer the ad – the car's original owner! As if that isn't enough, there are two witnesses you intend to call – one saw Ronnie driving the car at around 9.05 and one saw him getting out of it at his garage at about 10 o'clock.

You will be able to ask questions of all the witnesses. Ask for as many details as you like.

Prosecution witness 1: Ted Briggs

Last Wednesday 25 April, your red Mosquito car was stolen from outside your house. You think it must have happened around 9 o'clock in the evening because you parked it there at 8.45 and it was gone when you went outside to put out the rubbish at 9.10. A few days later, you saw an advert in the paper for a red Mosquito and answered it – the salesman was trying to sell you your own car! What an idiot! Of course he's guilty!

27 The law

THE TRIAL OF RONNIE SMALLS

Police officer
The defendant, Ronnie Smalls, a used-car salesman, is accused of stealing a car, a red Mosquito parked outside the owner's house last 25 April at 9.00 at night. The mistake he made was to put an advert in the paper to sell the car. Only one person turned up to answer the ad – the car's original owner! You came and arrested Mr Smalls at his garage after a phone call from Mr Briggs, the car's owner. This is the statement Mr Smalls made:

'I never stole any car. I couldn't have because I was drinking with my mate Reggie at the time. The car was sold to me by a man on 26 April. He didn't leave no name and address. I paid him cash.'

Prosecution witness 2: Mavis Wright
The defendant, Ronnie Smalls, a used-car salesman, is accused of stealing a car, a red Mosquito parked outside the owner's house last 25 April at 9.00 at night. The mistake he made was to put an advert in the paper to sell the car. Only one person turned up to answer the ad – the car's original owner!

You live opposite Ronnie's garage – not a very nice neighbour! You've had suspicions about that garage for a long time: a lot of sinister-looking characters hang about there. You saw Ronnie go out at about a quarter to nine. You were drawing the curtains of your top bedroom window at about ten past nine when you saw Ronnie drive the red car into the garage yard. You weren't at all surprised when you heard he'd stolen it.

Prosecution witness 3: Alex Fisher
The defendant, Ronnie Smalls, a used-car salesman, is accused of stealing a car, a red Mosquito parked outside the owner's house last 25 April at 9.00 at night. The mistake he made was to put an advert in the paper to sell the car. Only one person turned up to answer the ad – the car's original owner!

You live on the main road to Tamworth, a few streets away from the car's owner, and as you were walking the dog on 25 April you saw a man driving a red Mosquito. He screeched to a halt at the traffic lights, which were red. You walked past so you got a good view of the driver – you noticed him because he had been driving so fast. You're pretty sure it was Ronnie Smalls. The time was about five past nine.

Jury
The defendant, Ronnie Smalls, a used-car salesman, is accused of stealing a car, a red Mosquito parked outside the owner's house last 25 April at 9.00 at night. He then put an advert in the paper to sell the car. Only one person turned up to answer the ad – the car's original owner!

Listen to the evidence and then discuss the case to reach a verdict.

Defence witness 1: Sid Fellows
The defendant, Ronnie Smalls (a used-car salesman), who is a friend of yours, is accused of stealing a car, a red Mosquito parked outside the owner's house last 25 April at 9.00 at night. The mistake he made was to put an advert in the paper to sell the car. Only one person turned up to answer the ad – the car's original owner!

You want to stand by Ronnie, so say you saw another man driving the car at about nine that night when you were out. Don't let on you know Ronnie, though! Invent as many details as you like to make your story convincing.

Defence witness 2: Reggie Bragg
The defendant, Ronnie Smalls (a used-car salesman), who is a friend of yours, is accused of stealing a car, a red Mosquito parked outside the owner's house last 25 April at 9.00 at night. The mistake he made was to put an advert in the paper to sell the car. Only one person turned up to answer the ad – the car's original owner!

You know Ronnie took the car but he's a good mate and you're going to stand by him. Your story is that Ronnie came round to your house for a drink that night – he was with you at 9.00. Invent as many details as you like to make your story convincing.

Defence witness 3: Freda Sly
The defendant, Ronnie Smalls (a used-car salesman), who is a friend of yours, is accused of stealing a car, a red Mosquito parked outside the owner's house last 25 April at 9.00 at night. The mistake he made was to put an advert in the paper to sell the car. Only one person turned up to answer the ad – the car's original owner!

Stick by Ronnie. Say you were with him when another man came and sold him the car on 26 April. Invent as many details as you like to make your story convincing.

Judge
1 Tell the court the defendant's name and the crime he is accused of. Ask what he pleads: innocent or guilty?
2 Call the police officer who made the arrest to give his or her statement.
3 Ask the prosecuting counsel to question the defendant. Then ask the defending counsel to cross-examine him.
4 Call the following witnesses one by one in the order below. When each prosecution witness comes in, call the prosecuting counsel to question the witness; then call the defending counsel to cross-examine her / him. For the defence witnesses, call the defending counsel first, then the prosecuting counsel.

Prosecution witnesses:	Defence witnesses:
Ted Briggs (owner of car)	Sid Fellows
Mavis Wright	Reggie Bragg
Alex Fisher	Freda Sly

5 Remember what they said – take notes if you like.
6 Sum up – give a summary of what has been said. Tell the jury to go away and reach a verdict. You can indicate what *you* think if you like.
7 When the jury come back with their verdict, pronounce the verdict. If it is 'Guilty', hand out a sentence.

28 Education

PLACES

nursery	playgroup	primary school	secondary school	high school
comprehensive school	grammar school	college	university	private school
independent school	public school	state school		

DEFINITIONS

nursery	a pre-school (usually fee-paying) for children from birth to school age
playgroup	a group organised by mothers and play workers for children aged 3–5
primary school	a school for children under 11 years old
secondary school	a school for children aged 11–16 or 11–18
high school	a school for children aged 11–16 or 11–18
comprehensive school	a school for children aged 11–16 or 11–18, open to all
grammar school	a school for children aged 11–18 who are selected on the basis of an exam at 11
college	an educational establishment for students over 16, where they can study for academic or practical qualifications
university	an educational establishment for students over 18 who can study for a degree
private school	a fee-paying school
independent school	a fee-paying school
public school	a fee-paying school
state school	a non-fee-paying school

28 Education

PEOPLE AND COURSES

pupil	teacher	student
lecturer	course	subjects
lessons	lectures	tutorials
seminars	graduate	degree
research	A levels	GCSEs

OPPOSITES

strict	liberal	progressive
traditional	formal	informal
disciplined	free	bully
victim	shy	outgoing
insecure	confident	unpopular
popular	conformist	rebel

28 Education

COINCIDENCES

secondary school   bully

English   Mr Smith

Sarah   John   Maths

enjoy   primary school   university

goody-goody   strict

Manchester   best friend   Mrs Jones

freedom   interesting

London   hate   rebel

Liverpool   liberal

---

secondary school   bully

English   Mr Smith

Sarah   John   Maths

enjoy   primary school   university

goody-goody   strict

Manchester   best friend   Mrs Jones

freedom   interesting

London   hate   rebel

Liverpool   liberal

Intermediate Vocabulary Games
Pearson Education Limited © J Hadfield 1999

29 Relationships

EVENTS

fall in love	get divorced	go out with
get engaged	get married	live together
separate	break / split up	be attracted to
start a family	get pregnant	find a new partner
have an affair		

BEING TOGETHER

we stayed faithful	we trust each other	we've kept a sense of humour
we have a lot in common	he's calm and patient	she's very tolerant
we work at our relationship	we argue a lot	we grew apart
we lead separate lives	we get on each other's nerves	he drives me mad
she drives me up the wall	he's very annoying	she has irritating habits

29 Relationships

PEOPLE

1 husband	**2** wife
3 partner	**4** girlfriend
5 boyfriend	**6** ex-husband
7 ex-wife	**8** fiancé(e)
9 stepmother	**10** stepfather
11 gay couple	**12** lover
13 mistress	**14** single parent

29 Relationships

PEOPLE DEFINITIONS

married woman	married man
female half of an unmarried couple	one half of an unmarried couple
former husband after a divorce has taken place	male half of an unmarried couple
someone engaged to be married	former wife after a divorce has taken place
man who has married one's mother after the death or divorce of one's own father	woman who has married one's father after the death or divorce of one's own mother
either of two people involved in a love affair	homosexual couple
man or woman bringing up a child on their own	married man's extra-marital female lover

29 Relationships

WATCHING *COMMOTION STREET* (1)

1

You are an avid *Commotion Street* watcher. This is the basic set-up: there are seven houses in *Commotion Street* –

1 **Belinda** and **Anthony** live at number 1. Belinda is divorced from Leo, who also lives in the street, at number 7.

2 **Steve** and **Donna**, a happily married couple, live in domestic bliss at number 2.

3 **Elizabeth** and **Felix** live at number 3.

4 Their good friends **Greta** and **Harry** live next door at number 4.

5 **Ivor** and **Jasmine**, a couple in their early twenties, live at number 5.

6 The household at number 6 is not a couple. **Matthew**, who is gay, shares the house with **Martha**, who coincidentally is Steve's old girlfriend.

7 Number 7 is also a house-share: when **Leo** split up with Belinda, he moved into number 7 with **Nick**, an old friend.

The last episode you saw was episode 6. In that episode **Elizabeth** was talking to **Harry** at a party. He offered to drive her home. Is there something between them? You're dying to find out.

2

You are an avid *Commotion Street* watcher. This is the basic set-up: there are seven houses in *Commotion Street* –

1 **Belinda** and **Anthony** live at number 1. Belinda is divorced from Leo, who also lives in the street, at number 7.

2 **Steve** and **Donna**, a happily married couple, live in domestic bliss at number 2.

3 **Elizabeth** and **Felix** live at number 3.

4 Their good friends **Greta** and **Harry** live next door at number 4.

5 **Ivor** and **Jasmine**, a couple in their early twenties, live at number 5.

6 The household at number 6 is not a couple. **Matthew**, who is gay, shares the house with **Martha**, who coincidentally is Steve's old girlfriend.

7 Number 7 is also a house-share: when **Leo** split up with Belinda, he moved into number 7 with **Nick**, an old friend.

The only episode you have seen recently was episode 7. In that episode **Elizabeth** is having an affair with **Harry**. How did that start? What's going to happen? And **Jasmine** found out that she's pregnant. You're dying to know what happened next!

3

You are an avid *Commotion Street* watcher. This is the basic set-up: there are seven houses in *Commotion Street* –

1 **Belinda** and **Anthony** live at number 1. Belinda is divorced from Leo, who also lives in the street, at number 7.

2 **Steve** and **Donna**, a happily married couple, live in domestic bliss at number 2.

3 **Elizabeth** and **Felix** live at number 3.

4 Their good friends **Greta** and **Harry** live next door at number 4.

5 **Ivor** and **Jasmine**, a couple in their early twenties, live at number 5.

6 The household at number 6 is not a couple. **Matthew**, who is gay, shares the house with **Martha**, who coincidentally is Steve's old girlfriend.

7 Number 7 is also a house-share: when **Leo** split up with Belinda, he moved into number 7 with **Nick**, an old friend.

The last episode you saw was episode 8, though you missed episodes 6 and 7. In episode 8 **Elizabeth** is having an affair with **Harry** – you can't believe it! **Donna** told **Jasmine** that she and Steve are thinking of starting a family. And **Jasmine** told **Donna** she's pregnant, but the baby is **Nick's** not **Ivor's**! You're dying to know the rest of the story!

29 Relationships

WATCHING *COMMOTION STREET* (2)

4

You are an avid *Commotion Street* watcher. This is the basic set-up: there are seven houses in *Commotion Street* –

1 **Belinda** and **Anthony** live at number 1. Belinda is divorced from Leo, who also lives in the street, at number 7.

2 **Steve** and **Donna**, a happily married couple, live in domestic bliss at number 2.

3 **Elizabeth** and **Felix** live at number 3.

4 Their good friends **Greta** and **Harry** live next door at number 4.

5 **Ivor** and **Jasmine**, a couple in their early twenties, live at number 5.

6 The household at number 6 is not a couple. **Matthew**, who is gay, shares the house with **Martha**, who coincidentally is Steve's old girlfriend.

7 Number 7 is also a house-share: when **Leo** split up with Belinda, he moved into number 7 with **Nick**, an old friend.

The last episode you saw was episode 9 – you missed episodes 6, 7 and 8. So events came as a bit of a surprise to you! In episode 9 it seemed as though **Elizabeth** and **Harry** were having an affair – is that right? And **Greta** and **Felix** went out for dinner together. What on earth is happening?

5

You are an avid *Commotion Street* watcher. This is the basic set-up: there are seven houses in *Commotion Street* –

1 **Belinda** and **Anthony** live at number 1. Belinda is divorced from Leo, who also lives in the street, at number 7.

2 **Steve** and **Donna**, a happily married couple, live in domestic bliss at number 2.

3 **Elizabeth** and **Felix** live at number 3.

4 Their good friends **Greta** and **Harry** live next door at number 4.

5 **Ivor** and **Jasmine**, a couple in their early twenties, live at number 5.

6 The household at number 6 is not a couple. **Matthew**, who is gay, shares the house with **Martha**, who coincidentally is Steve's old girlfriend.

7 Number 7 is also a house-share: when **Leo** split up with Belinda, he moved into number 7 with **Nick**, an old friend.

The last episode you saw was episode 10, though you missed episodes 6, 7, 8 and 9. In episode 10 it looked as though **Greta** and **Felix** were having an affair. Is that right? Surely not! And **Ivor** admitted he was gay – to **Matthew**. And **Martha** has started going out with **Leo**. **Steve** finds this out and is really jealous! You are mystified – what has been going on?

6

You have never seen *Commotion Street* before but yesterday you turned on the TV and saw episode 11. You are completely muddled!

Someone called **Jasmine** burst into tears when a man called **Ivor** told her he was gay and was going to live with **Matthew**. Someone called **Donna** told **Steve** she was pregnant – but you saw Steve telling someone called **Martha** that he missed her. And you can't work out what is happening with **Harry**, **Greta**, **Felix** and **Elizabeth**. Who is married to who?

Can anyone help you understand what is going on?

29 Relationships

MAP OF *COMMOTION STREET*

Write the names of the characters underneath their houses.
Then draw lines to show the relationships between the characters. The first two have been done for you.

QUESTIONNAIRE

QUESTIONNAIRE

1   What qualities do you think make a good relationship?

2   What makes a relationship break up?

3   What qualities would you look for in a partner?

4   Getting married? Staying single? What are the advantages of each? What are the difficulties?

30 Space

STAR MAP

SPACE EXPLORATION

30 Space

HEAVENLY BODIES

sun	asteroid	moon	outer space
star	comet	planet	constellation
galaxy	atmosphere		

SPACE

1 rocket	**2** spaceship	**3** space capsule	**4** lunar module
5 probe	**6** astronaut	**7** space shuttle	**8** mission control
9 launch pad	**10** space station	**11** satellite	**12** UFO
13 flying saucer	**14** alien	**15** extra-terrestrial	**16** Martian

QUESTIONNAIRE

QUESTIONNAIRE

Space and you

1 Do you think money spent on space exploration is wasted?

2 What benefits do you think space exploration has brought?

3 What benefits could it bring in the future?

4 Do you think there is intelligent life elsewhere in the universe?

5 If you could buy tickets for a trip in a space shuttle, would you?

30 Space

MISSION IMPOSSIBLE

30 Space

STORY OF A MISSION (1)

30 Space

STORY OF A MISSION (2)

Rules sheets

4 The NHS
Rules
1 Play this game in groups of 3–4.
2 There are two sets of cards: Ailments cards and Remedies cards.
3 Put the ailments cards face down in a pile in the middle of the table.
4 Deal out all the remedies cards.
5 Look at your remedies cards, but do not show them to the others.
6 Player 1 begins. Pick up an ailment card from the pile. Pretend you are a patient. Tell the others what is wrong, e.g. *'I've got a terrible headache'*.
7 The other players pretend they are doctors. They can offer you one of their remedies cards and give you advice, e.g. *'You should take an aspirin'*, *'You need to go home and lie down'*, *'You need an X-ray'*.
8 The 'patient' (Player 1) can choose the best advice. Take your ailment card and the remedy card you have chosen and discard them (put them on the table beside you). If none of the remedies cards is suitable for you, just put the ailment card back at the bottom of the pile. (Patients cannot treat themselves!)
9 Then it is the next player's turn to be the 'patient'.
10 The 'doctor' who gets rid of all his remedies first is the winner.

6 Animal families
Rules
1 Play this game in groups of 3–4.
2 Deal out five cards to each player. Put the rest face down in a pile in the middle of the table.
3 Do not let the others see your cards.
4 Arrange your cards in 'sets' of three, e.g.
• lion, tiger, cat are all *cats*
• hamster, cat, dog are all *pets*
• canary, parrot, duck are all *birds*
• lion, tiger, dog all *eat meat*
• tiger, zebra, snake all have *stripes*
You can use any grouping you like.
5 Player 1 begins. Lay down your sets on the table and explain to the others why they are sets, e.g. *'I have a seal, a goldfish and a frog. They all live in water.'* Then you can ask any other player for a card to make another set. For example, if you have a sheep and a horse in your hand, you need another animal that eats grass to make a set. So ask one of the others, *'Anna, have you got any animals that eat grass?'* If the answer is yes, she must give you the card.
6 You can lay down your set if it is complete, explaining to the others why it is a set.
7 If the answer is no, or if you have no more cards in your hand, you can take another card from the pile.
8 Then it is the next player's turn.
9 The winner is the player with most sets at the end of the game.

11 Troubleshooting
Rules
1 Play this game in groups of 3–4.
2 Problems cards have words at the bottom. Solutions cards have words at the top.
3 Shuffle each set of cards separately, and deal them out equally to each player.
4 Look at your cards but do not show them to the others. If you have any pair of cards with the same numbers, you can put the pair down on the table in front of you.
5 Player 1 begins. Choose a problem card and tell the others about it, e.g. *'I can't save anything onto a floppy disk.'*
6 The other players can offer advice from their solutions cards.
7 Choose the player who you think gives the correct advice. You can check if the advice is correct by comparing the numbers on the cards. If they are the same then the advice was correct. If it was not correct, another player can offer advice.
8 The player who gave the correct advice can keep both cards and put them down on the table as a 'trick'.
9 The player with most 'tricks' at the end is the winner.

13 Gently does it
Rules
1 Play this game in groups of 3–4.
2 Shuffle each set of cards separately, and deal them out equally to each player.
3 Look at your cards but do not show them to the others.
4 Player 1 begins. Choose a picture card and ask a question about it, beginning *'How would you …?'* e.g. *'How would you shut the door of the baby's room?'* (You don't have to use the words on the cards.)
5 The other players can try to give an answer using one of the adverbs on their word cards.
6 Choose the player who you think gives the best answer, e.g. *'Quietly!'* or *'Gently!'*
7 If other players feel their answers were better, they can argue but they must give good reasons. There is more than one correct answer for each picture – it's up to you to choose the best! If you really cannot agree, call the teacher to decide.
8 The two players with matching cards can discard them (put them beside you on the table).
9 The player who gets rid of all her cards first is the winner.
10 As the game goes on, it will get more difficult to find an obvious answer for some of the questions. You will all have to be very inventive – e.g. *'I'm waiting at the dentist's angrily because he pulled out the wrong tooth last time!'*

Rules sheets

14 Strong feelings
Rules
1 Play this game in groups of 3–4.
2 Put the cards face down in a pile in the middle of the table.
3 Player 1 begins. Take a card from the pile and look at the adjective on it without showing it to the others.
4 Think of a person, object or place suggested to you by that adjective, e.g. *disgusting* might suggest a meal that you ate recently.
5 Mime a clue to help the others guess what you are thinking about and how you feel, e.g. mime eating something and looking disgusted.
6 The others should try to guess what you are thinking of and how you feel about it. They can ask questions to see if they are right.
7 You can only mime and answer 'Yes' or 'No'.
8 The player who makes the right guess can keep the card.
9 Then it is the next player's turn.
10 The player with most cards at the end is the winner.

19 Sensation snap
Rules
1 Play this game in groups of 3–4.
2 Shuffle the two sets of cards together and spread them out face down on the table.
3 Player 1 begins. Turn up two cards. If you can find a similarity between them, e.g. *'They both feel slippery'* or *'They both taste salty'*, you may keep the cards as a 'trick'. You can find any similarity you like to do with feeling (touch) and taste.
4 If you cannot find a similarity, leave the two cards face up.
5 Then it is the next player's turn to turn up two cards and try to find a similarity.
6 From now on, players can try to find a similarity between any two cards that are face-up on the table.
7 The player with most cards at the end is the winner.

18 Sound pictures
Rules
1 Play this game in groups of 3–4.
2 Shuffle the two sets of cards together and deal them out equally to each player.
3 Look at your cards but do not show them to the others.
4 If you have two of the same card you can put them down as a 'trick'.
5 Player 1 begins. Choose a card and tell the others about it, describing what you can 'hear', but not naming the things in the picture, e.g. *'I can hear something howling. What is it?'* or *'I can hear a rattling noise. Do you know what it is?'* Act worried, as if you don't know what the sound is!
6 The player with the same card can say, e.g., *'Don't be scared, it's only a wolf!'* or *'It's okay, it's only the baby shaking his rattle!'*
7 If this matches your card, you can keep both cards and put them down on the table as a 'trick'.
8 The player with most 'tricks' at the end is the winner.

20 Wow!
Rules
1 Play this game in groups of 3–4.
2 You have two packs of cards: Emotions cards (faces) and Situations cards.
3 Put the situations cards face down in a pile in the middle of the table and deal out the emotions pictures equally.
4 Look at your cards but do not show them to the others.
5 Player 1 begins. Turn up a situation card from the pile, e.g. *'You've done well in your exam'*. Try to find a suitable emotion card to match this situation (e.g. a happy face) and make a sentence to describe how you feel, e.g. *'I'm feeling so happy – I passed my exam!'* There is more than one possibility for each situation, e.g. *surprised, delighted, proud* and *relieved* are all possibilities for this situation.
6 If the group accept your sentence, you can discard both cards (put them on the table beside you). If not, you must keep the emotion card and replace the situation card at the bottom of the pile.
7 Then it is the next player's turn.
8 The player who can discard his cards first is the winner.

Rules sheets

21 Rivals
Rules
1   Play this game in groups of 3–4.
2   You have two packs of cards: Jobs cards and Candidates cards.
3   Put the jobs cards face down in a pile in the middle of the table and deal out the candidates cards equally.
4   Look at your cards but do not show them to the others.
5   Decide on three personality adjectives for each candidate in your hand and write them on the back of the card (e.g. *calm, confident, decisive*).
6   Player 1 begins. Turn up a job card from the pile. Say what the job is, and what kind of person you think is needed, e.g. *'We need an astronaut. We're looking for someone who is adventurous, confident and very calm.'*
7   The other players can suggest candidates from their hands, e.g. *'Tom here is very calm and decisive. You need someone decisive.'*
8   It is up to Player 1 to choose the best candidate.
9   The player with the best candidate can discard that candidate and the job (lay them on the table beside you).
10 Then it is the next player's turn to turn up a job card.
11 The player who gets jobs for all his candidates first is the winner.

22 Missed connections
Rules
1   Play this game in groups of 6–8.
2   You will need a board and one dice for the group.
3   Get into pairs. Each pair should choose a token (coach, train, ferry or plane) and take the set of six cards with the same symbol (e.g. coach).
4   Place your token on the correct terminal (one of the first four squares on the board, after HOME – e.g. the coach token starts on *coach station*).
5   Place your cards face down in a pile in front of you so that the card numbered 1 is on top and the rest follow in order 1 to 6.
6   The first pair starts. Turn over your top card (number 1) and read the instructions.
7   Then throw the dice to try to get the number you need. Each pair can throw the dice twice to try to get the correct number. You must throw the exact number you need.
8   Each pair can only move on to their own squares, e.g. if you have the coach token, you cannot move on to a train square.
9   If you do not throw the number you need, the turn passes to the next pair.
10 The cards will guide you round the board from HOME to DEPART, telling the story of your journey.
11 The pair who get to DEPART first are the winners.
12 When the game is over, each pair should tell the others the story of their journey. Who had the worst time?

30 Mission Impossible
Rules
1   Play this game in groups of 3–4.
2   You will need a board, a counter, a dice and a set of picture cards.
3   Put the counter on the square marked BLAST OFF!
4   Sort the cards into four piles – sun, planet, star and moon – and put the piles face down in the right places on the board.
5   Player 1 begins. Throw the dice and move the counter round the board.
6   When the counter lands on a square, pick up a card from the pile marked with the same symbol as that square, and tell the others about the event pictured on it, e.g. *'Oh no! Part of the space shuttle just broke off!'*
7   The group must decide what to do, e.g. *'One of us must go outside and mend it!'*
8   Then the next player should throw the dice and move the counter.
9   Lay out the used cards in a line to tell the story.
10 When all groups have finished, tell your story to someone from another group and listen to theirs.